ADDISON WESLEY LONGMAN HISTORY IN DEPTH SERIES

THE RUSSIAN REVOLUTION

TSARISM TO BOLSHEVISM
1861–1924

Graham Darby
Series editor: Christopher Culpin

LONGMAN

CONTENTS

THE RUSSIAN REVOLUTION

The Russian Revolution is an extremely complex event, made all the more complex by the varying historiographical traditions – Soviet, liberal, libertarian and revisionist – that have sought to explain it. At the heart of the Revolution there is a paradox: an autocratic, oppressive, bureaucratic and militaristic police state under the Tsars, was replaced by an autocratic, oppressive, bureaucratic and militaristic police state under the Bolsheviks. The system was the same, only the personnel had changed. This would imply that the Revolution was more akin to the original meaning of the word – 'a cycle, a recurrence of an event, a complete rotation', rather than its modern definition – 'the forcible overthrow of the established government, a great change'. In the modern sense, then, perhaps there was no revolution at all! Yet there was change as well as continuity – the Tsar, the Church, the aristocracy and even the middle classes (or bourgeoisie), were all swept away, and a new state was constructed, albeit on lines similar to its predecessor, but based on a revolutionary ideological philosophy.

Russia was a deeply divided society and each of the frustrated elements within it – the peasants, and later the industrial working class (or proletariat), the middle classes and soldiers – had different aspirations. The Tsarist regime was a peculiar institution, medieval in character, which managed to hold these disparate elements together – but only just. The modernisation of Russia undertaken after the debacle of the Crimean War (1853–6) only served to worsen existing tensions and to create new ones. These culminated in the so-called 1905 Revolution which, remarkably, the Tsar survived.

Mass discontent was rising again by 1914 and clearly some aspirations would have to be accommodated in the future. Nicholas II did not seem to be the man to do this. However, the aspirations of the various opposition groups were different and did not really constitute an alternative to 300 years of Romanov tradition. Accordingly, a revolution was not inevitable. On the verge of the First World War the regime was still intact.

It was, therefore, brought down by the war. A succession of defeats exposed the inadequacy of the government in general and the Tsar in particular. He was blamed for the defeats and he was removed. But he was removed by his own class not the people. February 1917 was an abdication designed to avoid revolution. The Tsar had held Russian society together; once he was removed there developed a climate of disobedience that gave full reign to the aspirations of the oppressed. The chaos that followed created a political vacuum into which Lenin and the Bolsheviks stepped, by means of a *coup d'état*. However, in order to retain control in the face of economic collapse and civil war the new regime adopted the oppressive governmental system of the old regime, and survived.

As you look through the outline of events in this chapter, think about the following questions:
- **Why was Russia such a backward, divided society?**
- **Could it have evolved into a more modern, harmonious society?**
- **How did the Tsar survive the 1905 Revolution?**
- **How stable was the regime in 1914?**
- **Why did Tsardom collapse in 1917?**
- **Why did the Provisional Government fail?**
- **How did the Bolsheviks achieve and retain power?**
- **Did Lenin betray the revolution?**

Chronology of important events

1853–6	Crimean War
1855	Accession of Alexander II
1861	Emancipation of the Serfs
1870	Birth of Lenin
1881	Assassination of Alexander II; accession of Alexander III
1892–1903	Witte becomes Minister of Finance; rapid industrialisation
1894	Accession of Nicholas II
1904–5	Russo–Japanese War
1905	Revolution (1904–7); October Manifesto
1906	First Duma; Stolypin becomes Prime Minister
1907	Second Duma; Third Duma (to 1912)
1908	Annexation of Bosnia by Austria
1911	Assassination of Pietr Stolypin
1912	Lena Goldfields Massacre
1912–13	Balkan Wars
1914	First World War begins
1915	Tsar becomes Commander-in-Chief
1916	Murder of Rasputin
1917	February Revolution: Tsar abdicates; October Revolution: Lenin and Bolsheviks replace the Provisional Government
1918–20	Civil war: Reds v. Whites
1918	Treaty of Brest-Litovsk; Tsar 'executed'
1919	Bolsheviks renamed Communists
1920	Whites defeated
1921	Widespread famine; Kronstadt Rising; Lenin introduces the New Economic Policy (NEP)
1922	Soviet state becomes the USSR
1922–3	Lenin suffers a number of strokes
1924	Lenin dies

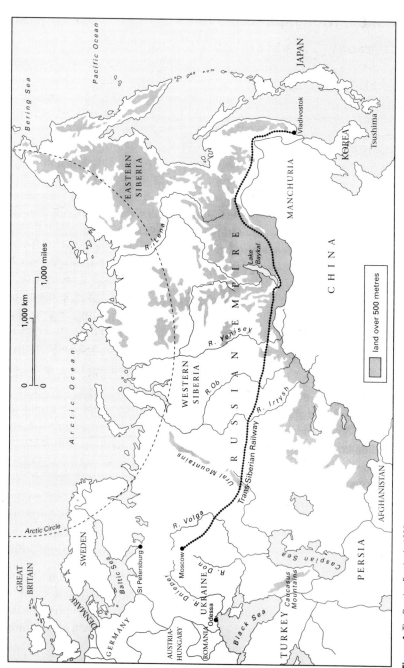

Figure 1 The Russian Empire in 1990

Imperial Russia

Geography, climate and agriculture

The Russian Empire was very large. So large, in fact, that it covered one-sixth of our planet's land surface. At its greatest extent it was 5,000 miles from west to east and 2,000 miles from north to south: a total of some 8.5 million square miles. It stretched from the arctic north to the deserts south of the Caspian Sea; from Poland in the west to the Bering Sea by Alaska in the east. It was both a European and an Asian country – in fact, the bulk of the empire (but not the bulk of the population) lay in Asia.

Despite its size, much of the Russian Empire was uninhabitable and its land unproductive. North of the Arctic Circle the land is 'tundra' and is too cold to support life apart from moss and some shrubs; south of the tundra lay the 'taiga', the largest forested area in the world. Much of this was cold and unproductive too, but in the warmer south-western region, farming was possible. To the south lay the steppe lands (a huge grassland plain) which can support some farming; but to the south of that, the desert and mountain regions of Central Asia could not. Only about 6 per cent of all Russian land could be used for farming.

The climate did not help either: it was very hot in the summer and very cold in the winter, the coldest regions being not in the north but in the east in Siberia. The soil was too hard to cultivate for much of the time. The result was an extremely short growing season (as little as 4 months in the 'taiga'), which was not helped by the uneven rainfall – low in fertile areas and high in infertile ones. The consequence of Russia's poor soil, unreliable rainfall and brief growing season was low yields. And the small surplus meant that crop failures – which occurred on average every three years – could produce subsistence crises. Yet the Russian population expanded dramatically in the nineteenth century, agricultural output increased (as the tables overleaf show) and cereals became Russia's principal export.

Population	
1815	40 million
1850	68 million
1864	74 million
1897	124 million
1914	170 million

Indices of grain production, sown area and yields, 1851–1914
(European Russia only; 1886–90 = 100)

Year	Production	Sown area	Yields
1851–5	68	92	75
1856–60	70	94	75
1861–5	71	94	75
1866–70	75	90	84
1871–5	81	98	83
1876–80	84	98	86
1881–5	93	100	94
1886–90	100	100	100
1891–5	109	99	110
1896–1900	120	105	114
1901–05	141	114	124
1906–10	142	117	122
1911–14	158	120	131

Taken from Peter Gatrell, *The Tsarist Economy 1850–1917* (Batsford, 1986)

How was this achieved? Initially it was achieved by putting more and more land under cultivation. However, by the 1880s there was virtually no virgin land left (this explains the land hunger that peasants increasingly complained about at the turn of the century). Yet the emancipated peasantry were able to rise to the challenge. Crop yields increased by as much as 50 per cent between 1860 and 1910 (by a greater amount in European Russia, as the table indicates). Aided by a greater variety of crops, agricultural output was able to keep pace with the rate of population growth. In fact, the peasants could not only feed themselves and a growing industrial workforce, but they also produced a surplus for export. It would be fair to conclude that the traditional view that sees Russian agriculture as stagnant and unproductive is simply not true.

Social structure

Russian society was structured like a pyramid (see Figure 2) – with the Tsar at the top and the peasants at the bottom. The vast majority of

Figure 2 A Russian cartoon of 1900. Above the workers are the capitalists: 'We do the eating' then the army: 'We shoot you'; the clergy: 'We mislead you'; and the royal family: 'We rule you'.

the Russian population were peasants, some 85 per cent even at the turn of the century. The geography and climate discouraged individual farmsteads, except in certain areas like the Ukraine. The short growing season of four to six months (as opposed to eight or nine months in western Europe) demanded bursts of intense, coordinated activity.

Hence collective farming became the norm. Encouraged by landlords and the state, the peasants had been organised into communes (in Russian, *mir* or *obschina*) since the middle of the eighteenth century and land was distributed in strips in an equitable fashion according to family size. This provided security and self-government; matters of common concern were decided by consensus and custom. In fact, the peasantry probably had more experience of self-government than any other social class.

The peasantry were largely illiterate, religious, superstitious and highly conservative. Their condition was supposedly a symbol of Russian backwardness. However, we must be careful not to underestimate the Russian peasant. Illiterate does not mean stupid. Our perspective is usually that of an observer from the Russian intelligentsia who made little attempt to understand peasant culture. The peasant, in turn, resented educated towndwellers with their western culture, values and dress (though they reserved most of their dislike for the noble land-owners). Recent research has indicated that the alleged poverty of the peasants was not so widespread; apparently their diet was superior to many of their European counterparts, and we have already observed that many of them were able to rise to the challenge of greater agri-cultural demand by adopting new crops and new techniques. There were also some signs of change at the beginning of the century as younger, now literate, peasants began to show less respect for religion and authority; and began to question traditional values. However, at the beginning of our period (the middle of the nineteenth century), most peasants were serfs – virtual slaves – with no personal freedom at all.

The rest of Russian society consisted of landowners, army officers, government officials, bureaucrats, clergy, professionals (such as lawyers, doctors and teachers), merchants, traders, businessmen and a very small working class. Indeed, both the nobility and the middle class were relatively small groups as well, but they possessed most of the wealth. An educated, privileged elite lording it over the vast majority was characteristic of any agrarian, preindustrial society. But this was now the industrial age and with industrialisation came dramatic social change, something that Russia would have to face if it was going to keep up with the other powers of Europe.

In addition to these social divisions, there were ethnic ones as well (hardly surprising in such a vast country). Russians only constituted about 44 per cent of the population of 125 million, as these figures from the 1897 census show:

Russians	55,650,000
Ukrainians	22,400,000
Poles	7,900,000
White Russians	5,900,000
Jewish	5,000,000
Finns	3,100,000
Germans	1,800,000
Caucasians	1,600,000
Latvians	1,400,000
Georgians	1,300,000
Lithuanians	1,200,000
Armenians	1,100,000

and over 13 million Turkic Muslims plus a variety of smaller groups.

In 1897 the non-Russian nationalities were not as yet a threat to the Imperial government, but the potential was there.

Government

The peoples of the Russian Empire were governed by one person, the Tsar. The tradition of Russian autocracy had sprung from Byzantium, the Eastern Roman Empire that had finally fallen in 1453. Russia's vastness would seem to lead to decentralisation and self-governing communities. But as the Russian population had expanded, more and more land had been taken over with the military help of the Tsar's army. Continuing colonisation over this vast area required continuing military protection and firm political authority. Later, Russia's power and prestige depended upon the ability of the Tsar's armies to preserve and defend this Empire. For over 300 years, from 1613, the Romanov dynasty held the country together.

The origins of Tsarism were therefore military and despotic. The Tsar's powers were absolute; there was no history of feudal contracts with the aristocracy, no give and take, no consultation – in fact the Russian aristocracy was quite weak. The Tsar exercised supreme and unlimited executive, legislative and judicial power. All policy- and decision-making lay with him. He was the 'father' of his people; they were his 'children'. The Tsar had ministers whom he could hire and fire and whom he consulted individually. He also had two advisory bodies – the State Council and the Senate. But the people had no say in government, no parliament, no political parties, no means of debate. The Tsar claimed his authority from God and this conception of divine-right monarchy was supported by the Church. However, it was a weakness of the Tsarist system that the Church was not as influential as it might have been, particularly at the parish level where it was seen as an arm of the bureaucracy rather than part of the community.

There was quite a gap between the claim of the Russian Tsar that Russia was his patrimony, and his means to enforce that fact. The difficulties of transportation and communication over immense distances, and in poor weather conditions, prevented the growth of a tightly-organised bureaucratic regime – until the 1860s when railways and the telegraph began to make this possible. His authority was accepted, but in practice the bulk of the country was run by the local landed gentry, clergy and bureaucracy. The land was divided into provinces which were sub-divided into districts, and further divided down to the village. In many ways, Russia was run as a colony with the bureaucrats as colonial administrators among an alien people. Given the gap between the peasants and the educated (as well as the gap between Russians and other nationalities), this analogy is quite a good one. The Ministry of the Interior, the police and ultimately the army kept order, and the Orthodox Church taught obedience and a better life in the next world.

Conclusion

1 Russia was different from western Europe. It did not share the same intellectual, religious or social traditions – even the alphabet was different. It was also partially Asiatic. You have to ask yourself the question, were western solutions to Russia's problems practical?

2 The only thing that the peoples of the Empire had in common was the monarchy. The Tsar held Russia together and he had to hold fast in the face of both external and internal threats. Accordingly,

Russia had to maintain its great power status: great powers that weakened went to the wall – disintegration and conquest were a real possibility. The only way to hold the Empire together, according to the government, was autocracy. What else was there? The very nature of autocracy implies the rejection of even the smallest encroachment upon it. Disturb the political foundation and would not the whole vast and ordered structure collapse in anarchy? It was that spectre of dissolution that made the Tsar continually refer to autocracy as 'inviolable' and 'immutable'.

3   The days when great power status was determined by the extent of territory and the size of population had gone. In the nineteenth century great power status could only be maintained by industrialisation and modernisation. Therefore Russia's survival as a great power required rapid economic modernisation – but modernisation undermined internal social and political stability. There was no easy way to reconcile the conflicting imperatives of domestic and foreign policy. In both areas, Russia was weakening. Internally the government could not rely on either the aristocracy or the peasants. Landowning nobles were weak and getting weaker in the later nineteenth century as they sold up and moved to the cities (60 per cent sold up between 1863 and 1915 because they could not make agriculture pay). Also rural conservatism could not be relied upon as increasing numbers of peasants became more and more dissatisfied – anti–noble, rather than pro–Tsar. The intelligentsia (i.e. educated Russians), too, were alienated as they had no civil rights, no say in government. The absence of any political forum precluded debate and this spawned a violent political culture in which terrorism and revolution were seen as the only alternatives to the autocracy.

There was no easy solution to the Russian dilemma.

◢ Source

The world should be surprised that we have any government in Russia, not that we have imperfect government. With many nationalities, many languages, and a nation largely illiterate, the marvel is that the country can be held together even by autocracy. Remember one thing: if the Tsar's government falls, you will see absolute chaos in

Russia, and it will be many a year before you see another government able to control the mixture that makes up the Russian nation.

Sergei Witte, Tsar Nicholas's Prime Minister in 1905–6

When the Tsar fell, chaos did ensue and the only way Lenin could reconstitute Russia was by re-establishing autocracy. In our own time with the passing of the communist autocracy, we have finally seen the disintegration of the Russian Empire. The communists were only able to hold it together for just over 70 years; the Romanovs built it up and held on to it for over 300. It is all too easy to dismiss autocracy as the obstacle to Russia's progress; Russia is still searching for the way to modernise within a viable political system. Clearly there is no easy answer.

Chronological survey 1861–1924

1 Alexander II's reforms

Defeat in the Crimean War (1853–6) impressed upon Alexander II the need to reform and modernise Russia's armed forces. He began by emancipating the serfs (giving the peasants their freedom) in 1861 and went on to pass local government and judicial reforms in 1864. Military reforms culminated in the law of 1874 and the new army performed quite well against the Turks in 1877–8. However, Alexander's reforms did not extend to political change and he was assassinated in 1881.

2 Count Witte and industrialisation

Tsar Alexander III (1881–94) did not approve of reform as he felt it undermined autocracy; however, he did encourage modernisation through industrialisation. This led to a dramatic increase in railway building and industrial production throughout the 1890s into the reign of Nicholas II (1894–1917).

Emancipation proved to be a disappointment to the peasantry, just as industrialisation created a discontented proletariat. The intelligentsia were also dissatisfied as their political aspirations were frustrated. Extremists favoured revolution and a **socialist** political solution; moderates preferred a **liberal** constitutional system.

KEY TERMS

Socialism is a political and economic theory in which the means of production, distribution and exchange are owned by the nation and wealth is distributed equitably. The state or the government controls industry, agriculture, transportation etc. – all the factories, farms, railways and shops. There is no private property and, therefore, no rich people and no poor people. Everyone works for the common good, rather than for profit, and everyone enjoys a similar standard of living. It is a theory sometimes summarised by the phrase 'from each according to his abilities, to each according to his needs'. Socialism is based on the theories of several writers, but most notably, those of Karl Marx (see Key Term, page 53).

Liberalism is a political philosophy based on the belief in progress, the essential goodness of mankind, and the autonomy of the individual. It means standing for the protection of political and civil liberties – in this context, the desire for a constitution, representative government, freedom of speech, freedom of association and freedom of the press. This was the political philosophy of the middle classes.

3 The 1905 Revolution

Failure in the war against Japan (1904–5) badly damaged the prestige of the monarchy in Russia. It presented an opportunity for the liberals to press for a constitution. When middle-class discontent joined with working-class discontent to create a general strike in October 1905, the Tsar, pressed by his Prime Minister, Witte, did finally concede a representative assembly, the Duma. The regime had come very close to collapse in 1905 but by making concessions and retaining the loyalty of the army, which crushed further unrest, it had survived. Very soon Nicholas and his new Prime Minister, Stolypin, were able to water down the constitution. Thus little changed and peasant, worker and middle-class discontent remained.

4 Russia on the eve of the First World War

Pietr Stolypin had passed a series of agricultural reforms, but these had limited effect. Nevertheless, the countryside was quite quiet at this time as there was a succession of good harvests between 1909 and 1913. In these circumstances, the regime was safe but peasant discontent had not gone away.

The considerable increase in armament production led to a dramatic increase in the proletariat between 1910 and 1914 and with it came industrial unrest. By 1914 the number of strikes was up to the level of 1905 but an attempt by the Bolsheviks (later the Communists) to bring the government down in the summer of 1914 was an abysmal failure. Nevertheless, discontent was considerable, and for both the peasants and workers there were no means of redress, no political outlet, no resolution in sight.

Russia's failure against Japan was followed by diplomatic humiliation at the hands of Germany and Austria over Bosnia in 1908–9. The upshot of this was that the regime was not going to be humiliated again and it embarked on an ambitious rearmament programme. However the programme was not due to be complete until 1917 so Russia was not ready for war in 1914 when yet another crisis blew up in the Balkans. Nicholas II felt he had to make some gesture of support to Serbia, but Russian mobilisation set off alarm bells in Berlin and led to war.

5 The First World War – defeat and abdication

The Russians proved no match for the Germans; a sequence of defeats and enormous casualties followed. Failure in war brought the regime to the verge of collapse and the government and the Tsar in particular were completely discredited. Strikes and mutinies created a revolutionary situation but in order to avoid a revolution, the generals asked for Nicholas's abdication in February 1917. However, the belief that things could get better once he had gone proved illusory. The Tsar, or rather the institution of the monarchy, had held Russia together; there was no satisfactory alternative to put in its place.

6 February–October 1917

A Provisional Government was formed as a temporary body until elections to a Constituent Assembly which would decide on the future constitution. Originally greeted with goodwill the Provisional Government forfeited its support by failing to distribute the land, control the economy or end the war. Moreover, the removal of the Tsar had created a precedent for disobedience which enveloped the whole country. Traditional authority had been dealt a death-blow. The fabric of society unravelled and the economy went into steep decline. The government was ignored and the people carried out their own agenda – peasants seized the land, workers the factories and soldiers would not fight. This was the real revolution. A political vacuum developed at the top; chaos below. Into this vacuum stepped Lenin and the Bolsheviks.

The Bolsheviks were insignificant in February and Lenin's return in April is only important with hindsight. The failure of the 'July Days' uprising by the Bolsheviks was a clear reflection of their weakness. However, by the autumn they had gained in strength and their position came to coincide with that of the people. Lenin seized power by a coup in October, by which time the Provisional Government under Alexander Kerensky was completely impotent.

7 Full circle: Bolshevik consolidation of power 1917–24

Basically, beyond capturing power, holding on to it and waiting for world revolution, the Bolsheviks did not have a programme. They were soon faced with civil war, threatened by various 'White' armies (as well as foreign intervention). But the civil war helped the Bolshevik Party to remain in power; it became centralised, authoritarian, bureaucratic and undemocratic. The Red Army defeated the Whites, who were in any case divided and even more unpopular than the Communists (as the Bolsheviks were now called). To win, Lenin ordered the requisition of grain ('War Communism'). This led to a collapse in grain production. Indeed the entire economy was on the verge of collapse, so in 1921 Lenin introduced the New Economic Policy which restored an element of *capitalism* – and it worked. Lenin himself suffered a series of strokes and died in 1924. By that time Communist dictatorship was established and the pattern set for Stalin's personal rule – though no successor to Lenin had been singled out. It might have been a new social order, but it was the old political system.

KEY TERM

Capitalism is the system whereby the means of production are privately owned and prices, production and distribution are determined by competition in a free market. This system is sometimes called 'bourgeois', a word which originally meant towndweller, and is most easily understood as 'middle class'.

ALEXANDER II, *1818–81*

Alexander II came to the throne during the Crimean War (1855). He first concluded peace and then initiated a wide range of social, economic, administrative and legal reforms. Despite earning the epithet 'Tsar Liberator' for giving freedom to the peasants, he had no intention of sharing political power and was assassinated by terrorists.

NICHOLAS II, *1868–1918*

The last of the Tsars came to the throne in 1894. Nicholas did not impress contemporaries; he was weak (unlike his wife Alexandra to whom he was devoted) and indecisive. He presided over defeat in the Russo–Japanese War (1904–5) and was forced to grant a constitution in response to unrest. Failure in the First World War led to his abdication in 1917. The following year he and his family were 'executed' by the Bolsheviks.

Sergei WITTE, *1849–1915*

From a family of Russified Germans, Witte became a civil servant in Odessa specialising in railway and transport matters. He became the director of the railways department in the Ministry of Finance in 1889, then Minister of Transport 1892, and Minister of Finance 1892–1903 where he presided over Russia's industrialisation. He then became Chairman of the Council of Ministers, a powerless position until he led the Russian delegation at peace talks with the Japanese in the USA (1905). Now his office was invested with power and as Prime Minister he was responsible for conceding constitutional government, the October Manifesto. He resigned from government in 1906 and did not hold office again.

PIETR STOLYPIN, *1862–1911*

From a landowning noble family, he too became a civil servant. Stolypin was appointed Governor of Grodno in 1902 and of Saratov in 1903, before becoming Minister of the Interior and Chairman of the Council of Ministers from 1906 until his assassination in 1911. Though a conservative statesman, he was prepared to work with a docile Duma and passed agrarian reforms to create peasant proprietors. He is generally considered to be Nicholas's last outstanding minister.

LENIN (Vladimir Ulianov), *1870–1924*

A law graduate and Marxist, he led the Bolshevik wing of the Social Democratic Party from 1903. He returned to Russia in 1905 but was in exile again from 1907 to 1917. Lenin returned to Russia with German help in April 1917 and issued his 'April Theses' but the failure of the July Days forced a temporary exile to Finland until October when he urged the immediate seizure of power. Framer of Soviet policy in the first years of Communist power, he made peace with Germany, ruthlessly suppressed opposition and founded the Communist International. He suffered a number of strokes in 1922 and 1923 and left no clear heir when he died.

TROTSKY (Lev Bronstein), *1879–1940*

Trotsky came from a Jewish peasant family and sided with the Mensheviks when the Social Democrats split in 1903. He was briefly Chairman of the St Petersburg Soviet in the 1905 Revolution but was arrested and exiled to Siberia. He escaped, lived in exile then returned to Russia in May 1917. Trotsky joined the Bolsheviks in July and played a leading role in the seizure of power. He was the founder of the Red Army and helped win the Civil War. The obvious heir to Lenin, he was considered too arrogant and too intellectual (and perhaps too Jewish?). He lost out to Stalin who had him expelled from the party in 1927 and assassinated in Mexico in 1940.

CHAPTER ONE

HOW MUCH DID RUSSIA CHANGE IN THE LAST PART OF THE NINETEENTH CENTURY?

Objectives

◢ To consider the causes of the emancipation of the serfs

◢ To consider the effects of this and the other reforms

◢ To describe the process and effects of industrialisation

◢ To consider political groups and the autocracy.

1860–63	Financial reforms
1861	Emancipation Edict
1864	Local government reform
1864	Judicial reform
1865	Censorship law
1874	Military service reform

After the defeat of Napoleon in 1815, Russia had emerged, along with Great Britain, as one of the two truly great powers. This pre-eminence had then come to an abrupt end with defeat in the Crimean War (1853–6). Russia's forces were found to be inadequate and its weapons outdated.

During the course of the war, a new Tsar, Alexander II, had come to the throne. He was determined to restore Russia's prestige by reforming its military and financial apparatus. Military efficiency seems to have been his principal concern since Russia's status as a great power was at stake. A thorough reform of the army – a new system of recruitment and the creation of a trained reserve – could only be achieved by emancipating the serfs.

Russia was an overwhelmingly peasant society, but the bulk of the peasant population had ceased to be tenants and had been turned into serfs in the sixteenth and seventeenth centuries. They were tied to the land primarily to prevent migration and depopulation and had become virtual slaves. In the census of 1858–9, there were nearly 23 million 'proprietary peasants' who were the property of private land-owners, over 27 million 'state peasants' and about 1.5 million 'household serfs' who performed domestic service.

Why did Alexander II emancipate the serfs?

Various explanations have been put forward for this momentous reform but there has been little agreement among historians. There is an *economic* argument – serfdom was inefficient and an obstacle to in-dustrialisation – but this has been called into question; serfdom seems to have been productive and industrial development does not appear to have been a government concern. There is a *moral* argument – serfdom was wrong – but this argument had been around for some time. More convincing perhaps, is the suggestion that *fear* was the main motive. There was growing peasant unrest – more than 100 serious local revolts occurred between 1848 and 1854. Alexander himself warned the nobility in 1856 that it would be better if emancipation came 'from above' rather than 'from below'. However, it does not seem that the nobles were convinced by this argument. What is clear is that Alexander himself wanted emancipation and in an autocracy the determination of the autocrat counts for a great deal. This probably brings us back to his wish to restore Russian prestige, by modernisation, by military reform.

The terms of emancipation

After several years of wrangling the **Emancipation Edict of 1861** gave the serfs their personal freedom and, in time, they were able to purchase land from the nobles in a process known as redemption. The government compensated the landowner and collected repayments from the peasants over 49 years. The land was not held personally but by the commune and members were jointly responsible for redemption payments. Statutes of 1863 and 1866 enabled peasants on crown lands and state peasants to redeem their lands on slightly more generous terms. A separate statute dealt with household serfs.

The effects of emancipation

No one was pleased with the outcome:

1 The **peasants** were dissatisfied: they ended up with less land than they had cultivated before (about one-fifth less – possibly more in fertile areas, less in infertile ones); they did not understand why they had to pay for it; many felt that the Tsar should have just given it to them. It was also not good value since the nobles kept much of the best land and the price tended to be above market-value. This was the cause of considerable resentment. Moreover, the binding of the peasants to the commune was not dissimilar to the old practice of their being tied to the nobility; thus peasant allotments were not private property in the western sense – they could be periodically reallocated or 'repartitioned' by the village assembly. This system meant that the peasants had joint responsibility for taxes and payment – this was an administrative and financial convenience for the state. But the elimination of the jurisdiction of the lord brought the discontented peasant into direct confrontation with the state official and, ultimately, the Imperial government. Indeed, hostility to 'masters' was a deeply-held serf attitude which lived on after serfdom.

Peasants continued to farm narrow strips in different fields. The idea behind this was to create an equal distribution of the best and worst land, but it was not efficient agriculture as peasants spent a great deal of time walking from one field to the next. (It also encouraged large families as the strips were distributed according to family size.) However, efficiency was not the objective, fairness was.

2 The **nobles** too felt resentment at giving up about one-third of their land. Many were unable to make agriculture pay and many sold up. There is no doubt that their interests were sacrificed. The landowners were compensated with political power at a local level through the Local Government Reform of 1864 (see below).

3 Thus **Alexander** failed to earn the gratitude of the peasantry, while at the same time he lost the devotion of the nobility. Peasant protests were widespread in 1861–3, but given the peasants' illiteracy and political unsophistication this did not represent a significant challenge to the autocracy. The level of unrest declined

and the countryside remained fairly peaceful for the next 40 years, though grievances over noble landholding never disappeared. And yet what is really rather remarkable about this reform is that an autocratic regime could be so generous, giving its peasants *both* freedom *and* land – after all, the United States gave its slaves freedom only, and at a slightly later date. The arrangements in Russia undoubtedly shielded the peasants from the usual dire social consequences of rapid capitalist development – vagrancy, underemployment and slum dwelling – while at the same time acting as a catalyst for an impressive growth and diversification of agriculture (see page 10).

Other reforms

The **Local Government Reform of 1864** created *zemstva*, representative assemblies at district (*uezd*) and provincial (*guberniya*) level. These were elected on the basis of property qualification and were domi-nated by the nobles. The *zemstva* had powers and responsibilities for such things as education, health, transport and the local economy. In 1870 the municipal reform created councils (*duma*) in the towns and cities. By 1875 *zemstva* had been established in 34 out of the 70 Russian provinces. Thereafter the process slowed so that only 43 provinces were covered by 1917. Nevertheless, these bodies did some useful work, particularly in education where the number of elementary schools increased dramatically from 8,000 in 1856 to 23,000 in 1880. Further, the existence of elected assemblies dealing with local concerns generated political discussion and awareness.

A series of **financial reforms** were passed early on. A single state bank was created in 1860, a unified treasury in 1862 and an excise duty on alcohol was introduced in 1863. In addition, a start was made to improve Russia's communications by building railways.

Like the *zemstvo* reform, the **Judicial Reform of 1864** was a necessary consequence of emancipation; the peasants now had legal identity – previously 'justice' had been at the whim of their owner. Western principles were adopted – such as trial by jury, equality before the law, an independent judiciary, public trials and so on, but the peasants were still subject to traditional customary laws in rural courts. The **Reform of Censorship (1865)** led to greater freedom of the press as the courts now had to decide if the law had been broken *after* publication. Universities were granted greater autonomy and a series of military reforms culminated in the **Military Service Reform of 1874**. The old system of drafting serfs to serve for 15 to 25 years was replaced by conscription by lottery for all classes. Men would serve for six years and would be in the reserve for a further nine. This new army performed quite well in difficult conditions three years later against the Turks.

Conclusion

Peter the Great had used western techniques to bolster Russian autocracy and Alexander II did the same. The question of whether reform and autocracy can co-exist is worth asking even today. What is clear is that reforms raised expectations for some and raised fears among others. These conflicting responses undoubtedly created political instability. Some intellectuals turned to revolutionary politics and terrorism.

What is ironic, however, is the fact that on the very day Alexander was contemplating (very limited) national political representation, he was assassinated (in 1881). Nevertheless, Gorbachev's failure in the 1980s to reform Soviet Russia 'from above' has served to place Alexander's reforms in some perspective. They now look quite remarkable. What they demonstrate quite clearly is that the tsarist regime *was* capable of examining its defects and implementing an extensive programme of reform. The problem was that in an era of rapid modernisation and change, this process had to be continuous. Unfortunately Alexander II's successors, Alexander III and Nicholas II, did not possess their forebear's vision. They placed their faith in reaction and repression.

Count Witte and industrialisation

Alexander III (1881–94)

Alexander III believed that his father's death demonstrated that reform and change of any kind were a mistake. Indeed, he attempted to reverse many of the reforms and began by purging ministers who were considered sympathetic to change. In the year of his accession he issued the Statute on Measures to Preserve National Order which was renewed every three years down to 1917; in effect, it turned Russia into a police state. A special police section, the Okhrana, was developed which concentrated on crushing political activity. Criminal cases were now conducted by military tribunal, censorship was much stricter and universities were brought under firmer control. In 1889 a new tier of provincial officials, Land Captains, was introduced with administrative and judicial powers over the peasantry. In 1890, the franchise to the *zemstvo* was restricted, as indeed it was to the *duma* two years later. At the same time the government orchestrated a vigorous campaign of Russification and antisemitism. All in all, this represented a very reactionary and repressive policy. However, one of the ironies of Alexander III's reign is that alongside all this reactionary policy he allowed considerable industrial development which naturally proved to be a powerful engine for change.

Now the peasants were free to marry and migrate, the population increased dramatically – in fact, it nearly doubled between 1861 and 1905 (up from about 76 million to around 140 million). This increased pressure on the land and released labour for industry. Nikolai Bunge, Finance Minister from 1881 to 1886, helped industry and agriculture by tariff protection and railway building. He established a factory inspectorate, reduced peasant redemption payments, established a Peasant Land Bank and abolished the Poll Tax. Foreign investment, which had been as little as 2.7 million roubles in 1850, now leapt to 215 million roubles by 1890 and railtrack increased from 1,000 miles in 1861 to over 20,000 by 1890. However, the real turning-point in Russia's economic development was the appointment of Count Witte as Minister of Finance in 1892.

The 'great spurt'

Count Sergei Witte was Minister of Finance from 1892 to 1903. He abandoned liberal economics for direct state intervention. 'A great power cannot wait', he declared and financed expansion by raising loans in Paris. He raised taxes, import duties (they had been dramatically increased in 1891) and placed the rouble on the gold standard (1897) to encourage investment.

It worked. The results were dramatic – between 1890 and 1900 coal production nearly trebled, iron ore was up three and a half times, petroleum two and a half times, while textiles doubled. Indeed 40 per cent of all industry in 1900 had been founded since 1891. The Russian rate of growth – 8 per cent per annum – was the highest in the world.

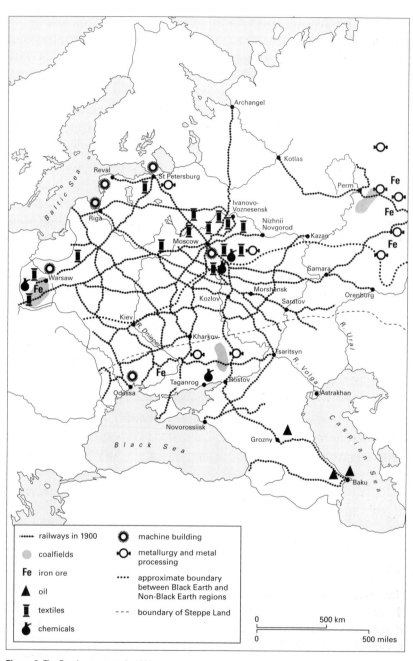

Figure 3 The Russian economy in 1900

By 1900 Russia was fourth in world industrial production. It was a railway-led boom with track mileage up from 20,000 miles to over 37,000 in the same period, a significant factor in a vast country with poor communications. The railroad linked areas of mineral production to centres of population and the internal market was stimulated. The most spectacular project was the 4,000-mile Trans-Siberian Railway linking Europe with the Pacific (see chapter 3, page 61 for a table of statistics covering industrial production and railway development).

This decade might well be described as the period of Russia's 'industrial revolution'. Although it was only a small proportion of the population, the proletariat (as the industrial working class came to be known) was concentrated in a few areas and in large factories (see Figure 3). In 1900 almost half of industrial labour was located in factories of over 1,000 persons. Living and working conditions were generally appalling. Hours were long (12–14 per day), accidents occurred frequently, wages were low (usually company vouchers rather than money) and accommodation was very poor (nine to a room was not uncommon). Discontent was rife. Thus to peasant discontent was added that of the urban industrial worker. The peasants wanted land and the workers wanted better conditions. The politically active members of these groups sought to fulfil their aspirations through socialist political solutions (see below).

The growing number of educated middle classes, on the other hand, favoured a liberal and constitutional political system that would give them a voice in creating a more efficient state.

The political groups
In the Tsarist autocracy politics as such did not officially exist. Nevertheless, that did not prevent the formation of a number of political parties at the turn of the century. Roughly, it is possible to identify three main groups – the Social Democrats, the Social Revolutionaries and the Liberals.

The Social Democrats
The Social Democrats were formed in 1898. They were a Marxist group which placed emphasis on the proletariat as the agents of revolution. It was not thought that revolution was imminent because Russia had not yet gone through the bourgeois phase. The party was formed under

George Plekhanov but it split in 1903 between the Mensheviks under Martov and Trotsky who were prepared for slow change and the Bolsheviks under Lenin who felt an educated revolutionary elite could speed up the process (see Key Term on Marxism, page 53).

The Social Revolutionaries (SRs)

This group was founded in 1901. It grew out of the Populist movement of Alexander II's reign which believed in a socialist society based on the collective ownership of land. There was no real unanimity in the party and it encompassed everything from terrorism to constitutionalism. It was led by Victor Chernov and later by Alexander Kerensky. The Social Revolutionary Party was mainly aimed at the peasants.

The Liberals

The development of the urban economy, the educational and legal systems and public services had generated a growing number of managers, engineers, clerks, lawyers, doctors, teachers, journalist *et al.* – in short, a growing middle class. These people were essentially liberal and believed in western-style constitutionalism. The Union of Liberation, an early liberal body, drew up its manifesto in 1904, but the principal liberal party, the 'Constitutional Democratic Party' (or Kadets for short) was formed in October 1905; their leader was Pavel Miliukov.

However, in the Tsarist autocracy there were no legal means of political expression; all power resided with the Tsar. In such a system the personality of the autocrat is of fundamental importance; in Nicholas II, Russia was not blessed with the greatest of leaders.

Tsarist autocracy

The Russian Tsar had absolute authority and he shared his power with no one. The Romanov dynasty had ruled Russia since 1613 and over time it had created an effective personal cult, whereby the Emperor was seen as the 'little father' of his people. 'Peasants cherished an icon of the ruler on their hut walls' claims historian Robert Service. The emperor's word was quite literally law. As we indicated in part one, the Tsar exercised supreme and unlimited executive, legislative and judicial power and he was supreme commander of the armed forces. Each minister was appointed by the Tsar and reported to him solely; the ill-named Council of Ministers in fact held no collective deliberations – each minister operated independently. The Tsar also appointed the governors who directed provincial government. Means of expressing unrest were limited and means of gauging it equally inaccurate. The Empire was governed by a centralised bureaucracy whose arbitrary authority was maintained by political police.

Nicholas II

Tsar Nicholas II (1894–1917), the last of the Romanovs, had few positive qualities. Contemporaries quipped that Russia did not need to limit the monarchy as it already had a limited monarch. Historians seeking to say something nice about him usually point out that he was devoutly religious, a good family man, and reasonable at organising picnics. He was, however, weak, inflexible and politically naive. At his accession the Navy minister described him as 'a child' (he was 26!) and lamented in an appropriately nautical analogy: 'what will be the course of the ship of state . . . the Lord only knows'.

Nicholas was not really interested in politics and he gave the great events of his reign little attention. The death of a favourite dog, on the other hand, he viewed as a major disaster. He wrote in his diary on October 20, 1902: 'the whole day after it happened I never stopped crying – I still miss him dreadfully when I go for walks. He was such an intelligent, kind, and loyal dog.' The shooting of innocent civilians did not elicit quite such a concerned response!

Recent historiography has been more sympathetic to the Tsar, suggesting he was not a dimwit but a convinced believer that only autocracy could save Russia from anarchy. The problem was that he *was* weak – his wife Alexandra who was made of sterner stuff (but equally bereft of political sense), constantly exhorted him to be strong. Nicholas was also inflexible – he lacked the imagination of his forebear Peter the Great and his grandfather Alexander II – and yet it was exactly this sort of imagination that was required to cope with the dramatic changes occurring within Russia.

Conclusion

In the census of 1897, Russia contained 2 million nobles (some urban, some rural), 700,000 merchants and professionals, 350,000 clergy, 14 million urban workers and over 100 million peasants. Russia was overwhelmingly rural, despite recent industrialisation. Thus about 85 per cent of the population were peasants, around 12 per cent were urban working class and some 3 per cent were urban middle class and aristocracy. Russia was, then, a land of considerable demographic imbalance and a land of dramatic contrasts.

◢ Source

A highly volatile mixture of ostentatious wealth and grinding poverty ... backwardness and modernity ... barbarism and sophistication ... advanced technology and primitive techniques; enlightenment and ignorance.

Alan Wood, **The Origins of the Russian Revolution** *(Methuen, 1987)*

It is perhaps remarkable that the regime was able to hold the country together at all. Quite clearly, Russian society was very different to that of the west and we must be careful not to assume that a western solution to its divisions and inequality was the answer. Perhaps the autocracy was the best way to hold a vast continent of peasants together. There was no real viable alternative to the monarchy at this stage, particularly given the political immaturity of the peasant majority; and a combination of the self-interest of the elite and effective repression ensured the regime's continuation.

Russia, then, was a divided society, an inequitable society, but it is difficult to see how those divisions could have been healed without reforming concessions – concessions which Nicholas II was not prepared to make. Peasant and worker discontent simmered beneath the surface; it would erupt in 1905.

Discussion

Here are four possible alternative courses of action which Russia could have adopted in 1900:

1 Maintain the autocracy – Nicholas's solution.
2 Tsar retains power but buys off peasant resentment by cancelling debts, worker resentment by welfare measures, and middle-class resentment by allowing a Duma with limited power – the 'Bismarck solution'
3 Shared power between the Tsar and an elected parliament based on a restricted (property) franchise – a liberal solution.
4 Real power to a democratically elected parliament with the Tsar as a constitutional Head of State – the British solution.

Questions
a What are the arguments in favour of each of these solutions?
b What are the arguments against?
c Which solution might have worked, and why?

For essay writing see the end of chapter 2 (page 51); for documentary tasks, see the end of chapter 3 (page 66); for notemaking, see the end of chapter 6 (page 127).

CHAPTER TWO

HOW DID THE TSAR SURVIVE 1905?

Objectives

◢ To consider how the regime survived the upheaval of 1905

◢ To consider its constitutional consequences.

Origins

As we saw in the previous chapter, peasant and worker discontent in Russia at the end of the nineteenth century simmered just below the surface and it would not take much to ignite widespread unrest. As it happened, from 1899 Russia was hit by a severe depression which produced unemployment and urban discontent. Towards the end of 1902 and during 1903 there were a series of mass strikes.

In the countryside, the situation deteriorated as well. In the 1890s rent strikes and attacks on private land had increased in intensity. The dramatic rise in population placed considerable pressure on the land. It has been estimated that the average size of peasant landholdings declined by 20 per cent. In addition, taxes had increased considerably and arrears had grown. In 1901 there was a serious crop failure and during 1902 there were major peasant uprisings. There was also nationalist unrest among the minorities in general and the Poles in particular. What we see here is a cumulative and complex pattern of social and political agitation which came to a head during Russia's unsuccessful war with Japan (1904–5). Just as the Crimean War had been a catalyst for change, this war would be too.

The Russo–Japanese War, January 1904–August 1905

The Russo–Japanese War owed its origins to Witte's Trans-Siberian Railway (see page 6). Russian ambitions to expand in the Far East brought her up against an equally expansionist Japan. In 1903 Russia annexed Manchuria. Japan tried to forestall conflict by suggesting spheres of influence – Japan would recognise Russia in Manchuria, if Russia would recognise Japan in Korea. At this point Witte was removed as Minister of Finance and 'kicked upstairs' to the ceremonial position of Chairman of the Council of Ministers, and Russian policy began to drift. Russia's failure to negotiate (the Russians held the Japanese in some contempt) convinced Japan that war was the only solution.

In January 1904 the Japanese laid siege to Port Arthur, sunk some Russian ships and bottled up the rest; on land they forced the Russian army to retreat. Port Arthur surrendered in December with 28,000 Russian losses; in February 1905 the Tsar's army was defeated at the Battle of Mukden with a further 89,000 losses. However, even greater humiliation lay in store. The Russian Baltic Fleet, which had sailed half-way round the world, was completely annihilated on arrival in the Straits of Tsushima in May. Despite its victories, Japan was by this time thoroughly exhausted and as Russia was in the throes of revolution, the two sides accepted US mediation and agreed to an armistice. The Treaty of Portsmouth (New Hampshire) was signed in August 1905. The terms were not too bad for Russia: Japan got Port Arthur; Korea was recognised as its 'sphere of influence' and Russia evacuated Manchuria – but there was no indemnity, and little loss of Russian territory. However, this treaty could not disguise the fact that the war had been something of a disaster for which the Tsarist auto-cracy had to take the blame. Moreover, long before the extent of the military catastrophe had come to light, disillusion and dissatisfaction had set in.

The Revolution – the course of events

Beginnings

It is very difficult to be precise about when the 1905 Revolution began and ended, but historians tend to agree that the upheaval spanned the years 1904 to 1907. A useful place to start would be July 1904 with the assassination of the Minister of the Interior, Plehve, who may or may not have advocated 'a short victorious war that would stem the tide of revolution' (depending upon whether or not one believes his rival, Witte). The general indifference to this shocking act was a measure of the fragility of the regime's popular support. Plehve's successor, Mirsky, favoured some reform and it was clear that the military reverses had put the government on the defensive; it was now considered incompetent as well as repressive and corrupt. But throughout 1904 the Russian masses were relatively quiet; it was the elite that made the running. Mirsky allowed a Zemstvo Congress to meet unofficially in St Petersburg in November. This had momentous consequences: the Congress's call for a constitution was followed by a banquet campaign – dinners were a cover for political meetings – and these events generated an atmosphere of political crisis. Nicholas wavered; he considered some form of representation in December but then rejected the idea. It was an opportunity missed; the regime would have benefited from moderate liberal support at this time.

Bloody Sunday

Then in December 1904 a major strike broke out at the Putilov arms works in St Petersburg and other factories struck in sympathy. By January 120,000 workers were on strike and news of the fall of Port Arthur only intensified agitation. Father Georgi Gapon, a priest and a union leader, planned a worker procession for Sunday 9 January to the Winter Palace in imitation of the banquet campaign, to present the Tsar with a liberal petition.

◢ Source

Today, at about 10 a.m., workers began to gather at the Narva Gates, in the Vyborg and Petersburg districts, and also on Vasilievsky Island at the premises of the Assembly of Factory Workers, with the aim, as announced by Father Georgi Gapon, of marching to Palace Square to present a petition to the Emperor. When a crowd of several thousand had assembled in the Narva district, Father Gapon said prayers and then together with the crowd, which had at its head banners and icons stolen from a Narva chapel as well as portraits of their majesties, moved off towards the Narva Gates where they were confronted by troops. Despite pleas by local police officers and cavalry charges, the crowd did not disperse but continued to advance ... Two companies then opened fire, killing 10 and wounding 20 ...

A little later about 4,000 workers who had come from the Petersburg and Vyborg districts approached the Trinity Bridge: Father Gapon was also with them. A volley was fired into the crowd, killing five and seriously injuring ten ...

Towards 1 p.m. people began to gather in the Alexander Garden, overflowing out of the garden itself into the adjoining part of Palace Square. The cavalry made a series of charges to disperse the crowd, but as this had no effect a number of volleys were fired into the crowd. The numbers of dead and wounded from these volleys is not known as the crowd carried off the victims.

The crowd then engulfed Nevsky Prospect and refused to disperse: a number of shots were fired, killing 16 people, including one woman ...

In the evening a large crowd assembled on Vasilievsky Island and began to build barricades in the streets ... It was fired on ... and two people were killed.

... In all some 75 people were killed and 200 wounded. It appears that among the dead are numbered women and children.

Quoted in Martin McCauley, **Octobrists to Bolsheviks** (Edward Arnold, 1984)

The police report underestimated the number of dead; the best estimate is that 200 were killed and 800 wounded. Contemporaries talked in terms of thousands killed and popular perception is in this case more significant than reality. After all, these were unarmed hymn-singing men and women. 'Bloody Sunday', as it became known, caused a wave of revulsion to spread across the country and it damaged the paternal image of the Tsar.

This event is usually taken as the start of the Revolution but as we have seen the government had already been under pressure for some time. Nicholas was not at the Palace to receive the petition but quite why someone could not have done so is a matter for speculation.

The wave of protest that spread across the land was led by the *zemstva* and by the end of January some 400,000 workers were on strike. At the beginning of February the Grand Duke Sergei, the Tsar's uncle, was assassinated and as the crisis grew it became clear that Nicholas had to make concessions. Finally, on 18 February, he proposed an advisory assembly and asked for suggestions. This led to a lessening of agitation but 60,000 peasant petitions poured in over the next few months. The Liberals formed the Union of Unions in May, an umbrella organisation for various professional groups, and this body set the pace. Any hope the government might have had of reversing the situation ended with the defeat at Tsushima. Now municipal councils were calling for reforms and *zemstva* and *duma* representatives met with the Tsar in June, though with little result.

Throughout the summer there was growing unrest and lawlessness. The police became increasingly ineffectual, strikes continued and workers became better organised as they came to appreciate their power. However, the initiative remained with the liberals who saw in a constitution a way of bringing about change without revolution. Government proposals which finally emerged in August were disappointing: a case of too little, too late. The Tsar proposed a duma, to be elected on a restricted franchise, but it was to be a powerless, consultative body. However, the conjunction of this concession and peace with Japan created a deceptive calm. It turned out to be the calm before the storm.

The October Manifesto

On 27 August Alexander Trepov, the Minister of the Interior, mistakenly granted universities autonomy and with the start of the new term, institutions of higher learning turned into political clubs as workers and other non-students were invited in. Unrest was rekindled and at the end of September a new wave of strikes broke out. Once the railway workers came out from 6 October the Empire came to a standstill. Food shipments and troop movements were frozen. The Union of Unions and leading liberals proclaimed full support. By mid-October Russia was in the throes of a general strike. Here was a truly revolutionary situation. Liberals and workers had come together and had paralysed the autocracy. But all this was very much unorganised, unplanned and unpredictable. Indeed, the leaders of the revolutionary left were taken by surprise. Yet over the nine months after 'Bloody Sunday' the lack of concessions from the government had made society as a whole more oppositional, and the workers in particular more politicised. This latter point was reflected in the formation of the St Petersburg Soviet (Council) on 13 October; this body became the strike headquarters and 40 or 50 other Soviets sprung up all over the country. The fate of the autocracy now hung in the balance.

Witte proposed real concessions in an effort to pacify the liberals and to avert revolution. On 13 October the Tsar agreed to a unified cabinet; next day Witte was appointed its chairman (and thus in effect became Prime Minister); on the following day Tsar Nicholas discussed the proposed concessions – the Manifesto – with his ministers; and finally on 17 October the Tsar agreed to and signed the document – not because he wanted to, but because he felt he had no choice.

◢ Source

We impose upon the Government the obligation to carry out Our inflexible will:

1   To grant the population the unshakeable foundations of civic freedom based on the principles of real personal inviolability, freedom of conscience, speech, assembly and union.

2   Without halting the scheduled elections to the State Duma, to admit to participation in the Duma, as far as is possible in the short time remaining before its call, those classes of the population which at present are altogether deprived of the franchise, leaving the further development of the principle of universal suffrage to the new legislative order, and

3   To establish it as an unbreakable rule that no law can become effective without the approval of the State Duma and that the elected representatives of the people should be guaranteed an opportunity for actual participation in the supervision of the legality of the actions of authorities appointed by Us.

*Quoted in Abraham Ascher, **The Revolution of 1905** (Stanford University Press, 1988), vol. 1*

The October Manifesto was greeted with demonstrations of joy by vast crowds and the workers began to go back to work. On 19 October the St Petersburg Soviet voted to end the strike. Liberals and workers were placated though few really knew what had been conceded by the Tsar. Although the political temperature dropped, there followed outbursts of irrational violence by right-wing extremists against Jews in the cities (with police collusion) and by peasants against landlords. There had been intermittent peasant violence throughout the year but really large-scale disorders broke out in October and November. Many peasants misinterpreted both the right-wing violence and the Manifesto as sanctioning attacks on landlords.

The government responded by halving redemption dues and promising their abolition as of January 1907 (this did occur). Nicholas was exasperated that the Manifesto had not brought the violence to an end and for a time Witte appeared to be at a loss as to what to do. However, when the St Petersburg Soviet called for another general strike in early November, it was ignored and the government took the opportunity to arrest its members (December). In the same month in Moscow there was a full-scale insurrection led by the Bolsheviks which was ruthlessly crushed by the army, resulting in over a thousand deaths.

This new ruthless determination to crack down was the result of the appointment of Peter Durnovo as Minister of the Interior. He was the 'man of the hour' and the government went on the offensive. Military expeditions were despatched to different areas and striking workers were shot. This policy of using small units to apply brute force indiscriminately succeeded in intimidating the vast multitude. Repression worked, but it did not reconcile differences.

Political developments

The year 1905 has been described as the 'apogee of Russian Liberalism', but the liberals were becoming uneasy about the extremism and violence. They had achieved a constitution (though the Tsar and his government studiously avoided that word) but were caught in the middle between the autocracy and the masses.

The Constitutional Democratic Party (Kadets) held its founding congress in Moscow in October and later Shipov and Guchkov formed the Union of October 17 (Octobrists) which represented a more conservative liberalism. To the right, ultra conservatives founded the Union of Russian People (URP) to defend autocracy, though ultimately the fate of the autocracy depended on the loyalty of the country's military forces. There were a number of mutinies in the forces during the revolution but they tended to be self-contained affairs, concerned with local conditions. The most famous mutiny, that of the battleship *Potemkin* in June was more of an embarrassment than a threat, though unrest in Odessa with which it was associated did lead to over 2,000 deaths. The most serious mutinies actually came late in 1905 and in the summer of 1906. They were largely a response to slow demobilisation. At no time did they coincide with the greatest outbursts of urban discontent; and in any event were defused by government concessions.

On 24 November the government abolished censorship and on 11 December issued the Electoral Law. This consisted of an elaborate, indirect voting system (as Figure 4 shows) whereby most of the people voted for representatives who in turn voted for others, and so on, so that a single gentry vote came to be worth two burger votes, 15 peasant votes and 45 worker votes. It was believed that this system would produce a docile and loyal chamber.

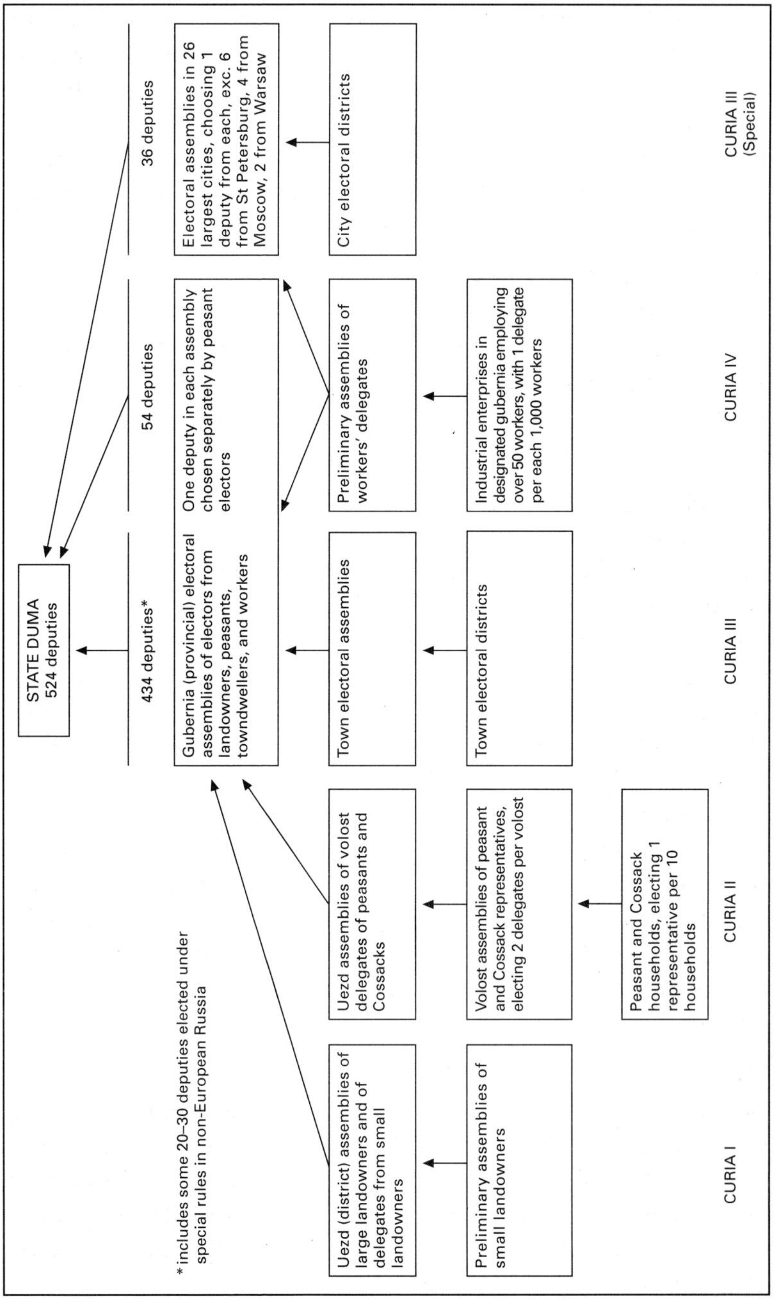

Figure 4 The electoral system after the Electoral Law 1905

* includes some 20–30 deputies elected under special rules in non-European Russia

STATE DUMA
524 deputies

434 deputies*

Gubernia (provincial) electoral assemblies of electors from landowners, peasants, towndwellers, and workers

Uezd assemblies of volost delegates of peasants and Cossacks

Volost assemblies of peasant and Cossack representatives, electing 2 delegates per volost

Peasant and Cossack households, electing 1 representative per 10 households

Uezd (district) assemblies of large landowners and of delegates from small landowners

Preliminary assemblies of small landowners

Town electoral assemblies

Town electoral districts

CURIA I

CURIA II

CURIA III

54 deputies

One deputy in each assembly chosen separately by peasant electors

Preliminary assemblies of workers' delegates

Industrial enterprises in designated gubernia employing over 50 workers, with 1 delegate per each 1,000 workers

CURIA IV

36 deputies

Electoral assemblies in 26 largest cities, choosing 1 deputy from each, exc. 6 from St Petersburg, 4 from Moscow, 2 from Warsaw

City electoral districts

CURIA III
(Special)

Since January it had become clear that the revolutionary upheaval was essentially an unpredictable and spontaneous affair. Neither the government nor the leaders of the opposition controlled the drift of events. Many people remained moderate and did not wish to over-throw the Tsar, but as they entered 1906 no one was quite sure whether the revolution was in retreat or whether it would flare up again. The Tsar had reluctantly made concessions, but he could not rescind them – he could not turn the clock back. A political process was in motion and worker and peasant activism was sustained by the political parties, who were gearing up for the elections.

In 1906 and 1907 there was greater lawlessness and political terror than before but mass protests and mass violence declined as the political struggle switched to the Duma. The government itself con-tinued to drift, alternating between reform and repression. Nicholas was, of course, as indecisive as ever – 'weak on everything except the autocracy' as the British ambassador put it; Witte too seems to have been ambivalent about the constitutional path. He was in an in-creasingly weak position. Although with hindsight he is considered a man of stature, contemporaries completely mistrusted him (Nicholas called him 'a chameleon') and believed that he was motivated solely by self-interest. The Tsar did not like him and nor did the opposition. Witte's position was becoming impossible. Since he had saved the monarchy he was now dispensable as well. Resolute policy, as we have indicated, was dictated by the Interior Minister, Peter Durnovo. He issued sweeping directives to crush opposition by a campaign of ex-tensive repression (arrests and executions) to counter the Social Revolutionaries' assassination campaign launched at the end of 1905 and aimed at police and government officials. (It is estimated that 4,000 government officials and police were either killed or wounded in 1906–7.) Durnovo placed about two-thirds of Russia's provinces under some form of martial law and cracked down on the press.

Against Witte's advice, on 20 February 1906 the Tsar issued laws up-grading the State Council (an old advisory body) to the status of a 198-member second chamber (an upper chamber – like our House of Lords) with the power of veto. Half its members would be appointed by the Tsar for life, the other half would be elected by nobles, *zemstvo* assemblies, the Holy Synod and so on. The October Manifesto had referred to only one legislative body – the State Duma – and this was clearly a contravention of that commitment. It demonstrated the Tsar's desire to undermine the constitutional experiment.

Despite this setback the elections for the Duma began at the end of February 1906 and in most places had ended by mid-April, though in some they were not complete by the time of dissolution! On 4 March the government granted the Right of Assembly and Union which in effect legalised political parties and trade unions. However, parties to the left of the Kadets (the Social Democrats and Social Revolutionaries) decided to boycott the elections. This was a mistake: they seriously misjudged the mood of the people who were keen to exercise their franchise.

Witte resigns

Witte did not remain in office to witness the opening of the Duma, but resigned with effect from 22 April. For some time, his position had become untenable but he hung on to negotiate an important foreign loan that ensured that the government could meets its commitments and pay the forces of law and order. His 'unprincipled vacillation between liberalism and reaction', as a contemporary critic described it, left him discredited in the eyes of many. Witte himself had wearied of the constant criticism. But it removed a powerful presence at a crucial time; 'his influence had been enormous in shaping the Empire's economic revolution and the changes in its political institutions' (Abraham Ascher). Witte had steered the monarchy through its most perilous hour. However, his arrogance had left him friendless. He was replaced by Ivan Goremykin and his rival at the Interior Ministry, Durnovo, was replaced by Pietr Stolypin (of whom more later).

The Fundamental Laws

A day later the government issued the Fundamental Laws, which provided a detailed framework for the operation of the government, under the new constitution – though that word was not used. It was a strikingly conservative document and although it seemed to comply with the October Manifesto, it was a far cry from the aspirations of liberal society. The Tsar could veto any legislative measures, dissolve the Duma prior to its five-year term and under article 87, issue laws when the Duma was in recess. The Tsar retained control of the administration of the Empire, determined foreign policy, commanded the armed forces, appointed all ministers and could declare a state of emergency. Moreover, the Duma was also circumscribed by the State Council and its power over the budget was considerably watered down by taking away its right to discuss many financial matters.

Yet members of the Duma had the right of free speech, parliamentary immunity and the right to question Ministers. There is no doubt that from April 1906 to February 1917 the body did provide a forum for criticism of the regime. In this sense, it did undermine the autocracy and came to be seen as a possible alternative to it. However, it was a long way from the type of constitutional monarchy that many felt the revolution had achieved and therefore further political change was a priority for many of the delegates.

The First Duma (27 April–9 July 1906)

The government was stunned by the results of the election. The masses turned out to be neither conservative nor revolutionary but they did want change, and the results reflected the deep feeling of resentment against the government felt by all classes. It is difficult to be precise about the composition of the Duma because many deputies changed their allegiances during its course; however, these figures indicate affiliations when 478 deputies had been elected:

Kadets (and allies)	185
Non-partisans*	112
Socialists (SRS and SD)	17
Trudoviki (Labour Group)[†]	94
Progressives of Peasant Reps	25
Poles	32
Octobrists	13

* Principally peasants
† This was a political group created by the First Duma which was composed of a number of peasant deputies and radical intellectuals who demanded democracy and land nationalisation.

The First Duma was opened in an elaborate ceremony on 27 April 1906. The American ambassador recorded the proceedings:

◢ Source

In the throne room of the Winter Palace there was an assemblage of people different from any that has ever taken place in the history of Russia. On the left of the throne, taking up the entire left side of the hall, were the members of the Duma, in every conceivable costume, the peasants in rough clothes and long boots, merchants and trades people in frock coats, lawyers in dress suits, priests in long garb and almost equally long hair, and even a Catholic bishop in violet robes.

On the opposite side of the hall were officers in braided uniforms, courtiers covered with decorations, Generals, members of the Staff and members of the Imperial Council of Russia.

In watching the deputies I was surprised to note that many of them did not even return the bows of His Majesty, some giving an awkward nod, others staring him coldly in the face, showing no enthusiasm, and even almost sullen indifference. As he rose again from the throne, there was an absolute stillness. He then proceeded in a firm voice to read his address. When he finished there was a tremendous outbreak of applause, but limited almost entirely to the right side of the hall, the deputies remaining quiet. As he descended from the throne and the members of the Royal Household formed in line according to their rank, the applause and shouting on the right continued and increased, but the marked silence on the left was ever noticeable. . . . the contrast between those on the left and those on the right was the greatest that one could possibly imagine, one being a real representation of different classes of this great Empire, and the other of what the autocracy and bureaucracy has been.

The US Ambassador, quoted in Abraham Ascher, **The Revolution of 1905**
(Stanford University Press, 1992), vol. 2

The opening ceremony was a public relations disaster.

The First Duma was dominated by the Kadets. They felt confident in pressing their demands because they believed the regime would collapse if it ordered a dissolution. Among other things they called for the abolition of the law of 1881 on emergency regulations; the elimination of the State Council; universal suffrage; the abolition of capital punishment; amnesty for political prisoners; a ministry enjoying the confidence of the majority of the Duma; and the compulsory seizure of private land. In effect, they demanded that the Duma became a sovereign legislative body; but the delegates were overconfident.

As early as mid-May the Council of Ministers decided that the legislature would have to be dissolved. The only question was timing. The deputies anticipated violence from below and the government nervously assessed the situation. Serious disorders began in early May affecting much of the countryside, some cities and the army. Was this the last gasp of the revolution or did it herald the collapse of the regime? It is always important to remember that contemporaries had no idea what was to come.

Despite the unrest in the countryside in 1905, the peasants had had no influence on the development of the revolution thus far, but in 1906 they were more prominent. Their primary aim was to gain more land: in European Russia in 1905, 100,000 nobles owned one-third of arable land while 12 million peasant households shared the rest. Another bad harvest was the background to the unrest but there is evidence that the peasants were becoming increasingly politicised and many placed great faith in the Duma. By July the unrest had pretty much run its course, though the peasants were far from content.

The industrial proletariat, which had been so critical a force in the last three months of 1905, played a less important role in 1906, not helped by the fact that its political parties had boycotted the Duma. The crushing of the uprising in Moscow in December 1905 seems to have been a decisive factor in dampening the spirit of militancy, though there was a significant campaign against the rise of unemployment.

Lawlessness of various kinds – political terrorism, criminality and right-wing hooliganism (usually antisemitic) remained at a high pitch in 1906, but the government could continue to rely on the army to restore order. There were a number of mutinies – 153 between April and July – but once again these were isolated events mainly concerned with conditions of service, and in no way coordinated with other unrest. The vast majority of soldiers continued to obey orders.

The major question for the government was which of the two – the dissolution or the continuation of the Duma – would stimulate greater unrest? The government played for time. By July the Duma had become more militant, passing an 'Appeal to the People' for the expropriation of private land, but the unrest in the country began to subside. Finally, the Tsar resolved to dissolve the Duma and replace Goremykin with Stolypin. Troop numbers were built up to 22,000 in St Petersburg and the Duma was dissolved in the middle of the night on 8/9 July when no one was there. The government promised that another Duma would meet on 20 February 1907. The Deputies were taken by complete surprise.

The Kadet group immediately decided to issue a manifesto directly to the people. On 10 July the deputies issued the **Vyborg Manifesto** (which was ultimately signed by 230 – mainly Kadets and Trudoviki). They called upon the people to suspend the payment of taxes – but no one responded. That is not to say that the people were indifferent to the Duma's dissolution, but after 18 months of agitation the momentum had slackened and the Manifesto failed to spark an up-rising. The Kadets had miscalculated; the government had judged the mood better. And the government now had an outstanding Prime Minister, Pietr Stolypin. The tide had turned.

Stolypin

On taking office Stolypin stated 'the Revolution must be suppressed' though he also believed in reform. The continuing terrorism, including an attack on the Prime Minister, led Stolypin to agree to the establishment of Field Courts-Martial on 19 August, whereby military tribunals could deal with cases without investigation or delay. Between August 1906 and April 1907 when the law lapsed, 1,144 people were executed by these courts (and over 2,000 by ordinary courts over a longer period). Later, in November 1907, a Duma deputy coined the phrase 'Stolypin necktie' to characterise the noose – and the jibe stuck.

Repression worked and in October 1906 the British ambassador stated 'public opinion is not [as] revolutionary as it was a year ago' though he conceded that this did not mean people were any more reconciled to the continuation of the regime. Stolypin's crackdown did not simply consist of executions, there were searches and arrests (1,400 in Warsaw alone in one day), the press was muzzled and the Kadets were targeted (especially the Vyborg deputies).

Another dimension of Stolypin's approach was agrarian reform and his measures were passed by decree on 9 November 1906 (for an assessment of these reforms see chapter 3). He also worked hard to influence the elections for the next Duma. The Kadets were outlawed, the Octobrists and the extreme right (Union of Russian People) were supported by financial help and the opposition was harassed by dispersing meetings and tampering with the electoral roll. But all this was to no avail. The Second Duma turned out to be even more radical than the first, more political and more polarised. What the elections did demonstrate was the continuing faith of the masses in the electoral process, in the Duma.

The Second Duma (20 February– 2 June 1907)

The deputies' affiliations are thought to have been as follows:

Social Democrats – Mensheviks	47
Social Revolutionaries (SRs)	37
Popular Socialists	16
Trudoviki	104
Peaceful Renewal Party	28
Kadets	91
Octobrists	42
Rightists	10
National Parties	93
Non Party	50

Once again the government was shocked. Once again the Tsar and his Prime Minister were soon exasperated by (what they felt to be) the intemperate language of the deputies. Stolypin indicated that he would work with the Duma, but left-wing deputies (and there were now over 200 of those since the Socialists had abandoned their boy-cott) would not work with him. A stalemate ensued and, within the chamber, right- and left-wing deputies engaged in slanging matches. On 16 April, a deputy named Zurabov attacked the army; this caused outrage and although the incident was overcome, the Tsar now decided on dissolution, pending a new electoral law. The government knew that it could not dispense with the Duma altogether, but it had to find a way to make it docile.

In April and May peasant disturbances occurred again and the deputies in the Duma voted to nationalise the land. Once it became obvious by late May that the deputies would not support his agrarian reforms, Stolypin looked for a pretext to dissolve the chamber. He had also received two detailed police reports that indicated that the country was now calm. On 1 June he ordered the arrest of some Social Democrats who were committed to the violent overthrow of the regime. At 6 a.m. on Sunday 3 June 1907 the Second Duma was dissolved. There were some arrests in the aftermath but for the most part the country was quiet and the deputies simply went home. The dissolution was met by apathy, disillusion and despair.

On the same day the government announced a new **Electoral Law**. The new law was really the old law with numerous changes – in the number of seats assigned to particular regions, social groups and ethnic minorities. It was complex but transparent. The outlying regions lost out and the franchise arrangements were heavily weighted in favour of the landowners. It has been estimated that about 1 per cent of the electorate now elected 300 out of the 442 deputies. Needless to say, the Third Duma, which met in November 1907, was a much more compliant and conservative assembly.

Was this a *coup d'état* as opponents claimed? The dissolution and the Electoral Law represent the end of the revolution. The main achievement of the upheaval was that 3 June subverted 17 October. The people had not proved to be sufficiently conservative for the regime so Stolypin determined to give them less voice. The opposition was demoralised and defeated. Now the government could pick it off on a piecemeal basis. Many came to feel that nothing had been achieved, but 1907 was not 1904, and the regime's unpopularity had, if anything, increased. Would the government use its victory to seek reconciliation?

Analysis

So how had the regime survived? As you can now appreciate, the revolution was such a complex sequence of events that there is no easy answer. However, some points stand out.

1 The unrest did not constitute a systematic attack on tsardom.
There was no real attempt to put forward a viable alternative to

300 years of Romanov tradition. Much of the opposition was moderate, not revolutionary – in fact the revolutionary left was taken by surprise and was wholly unprepared. The unrest was spontaneous and stretched out over time (reflecting the vastness and variety of the Russian Empire) and it lacked leadership, direction and unity of purpose. The various groups – workers, liberals, peasants, soldiers, students, nationalists – did not agitate at the same time; they did not coordinate their activities. Peasant and ethnic unrest assumed a rhythm all its own and the mutinies did not coincide with the most dramatic periods of political activism. People's motives were often different and did not coincide with those of the politicians. In many cases, motives were economic rather than political – peasants wanted land, workers and soldiers better conditions. It is clear that the liberals led the way in their demand for a constitutional monarchy, and when their agitation coincided with that of the proletariat in October 1905 (the only time the two groups came together), the autocracy was visibly shaken; but when the workers attempted to rise up on their own (as in Moscow in December 1905) they were easily put down. Their militancy unnerved many moderates, and students and bourgeoisie subsequently placed their faith in the Duma; but the regime had little difficulty in circumscribing this body, as the deputies overestimated their strength and importance, and made no attempt to develop cooperative government. Had there been some attempt at cooperation on their part, the regime would have found it more difficult to dissolve the body. As Abraham Ascher suggests 'The lack of political maturity among all social groups undermined every endeavour to reach a reasonable solution'.

2   The government made timely concessions to weather the storm and to divide the opposition. The October Manifesto – the granting of a constitution – may well have saved the monarchy from total collapse. Witte's timely intervention detached the liberals from the workers (and indeed moderate workers from militants) and held out the promise of participatory politics. Although Witte lost his way after this, he did at least negotiate an important loan which was probably just as important in saving the monarchy as was the Manifesto. Timely concessions were also

made to other groups; for instance, mortgage relief (and ultimately abolition) for the peasants (in November 1905) and the promise of better conditions for the armed forces.

3   The government at times showed resolute determination to survive. Nicholas himself was determined to make as few concessions as possible and subsequently backtracked on as many of those as possible. Nicholas believed that too many concessions would only lead to greater dissatisfaction and the demand for more (who is to say he was wrong?). He also believed that because of Russia's size and variety, only the autocracy could hold it together.

The key to the regime's survival, of course, was its use of repression and ultimately the loyalty of the army. Fortunately for the Tsar the war with Japan – which started off the whole series of upheavals – proved to be short and limited in its effect. Despite mutinies, the vast majority of soldiers remained loyal to the regime – and the opposition could not match the weaponry and organisation of the army as the Moscow uprising demonstrated. In addition, the government was well served by Durnovo and Stolypin who applied repression – arrests, imprisonment, executions – mercilessly. The government countered terror with terror. This policy did not win the regime any friends but it was effective – and in any case many moderates were unnerved by opposition extremists and were prepared to tolerate this sort of response. Also Nicholas and Stolypin were not prepared to be browbeaten by the Duma – they were not afraid to dissolve it and ultimately they were not afraid to water down the constitution.

Conclusion

The regime had survived with much of its powers intact. Was 1905 in fact a revolution? Did it achieve anything? As we have said before 1907 was not 1904: the Tsar could not put the clock back completely. Although the regime had won, the Duma remained a forum for criticism; and multiparty politics, however restricted, did exist. Newspapers had more freedom and unions did not vanish completely. The regime had been put on warning; it now had an opportunity to evolve.

Was 1905 'a dress rehearsal' for 1917, as Lenin put it? 1905 did not inevitably lead to 1917, but the same tensions which emerged in 1905 did surface again in 1917: the economic condition of the peasants; the conflict between workers and industrialists; and the demand for civil rights among the middle classes. There were also the demands by those in the armed forces for better conditions of service, and by national groups for cultural and political autonomy. In short, the Russian people was now more aware of its dissatisfaction and more political in its approach to a solution. How could the regime satisfy all these grievances? Was it an impossible task or was there a *via media* (a middle way)?

Postscript – nationalities and revolutionaries

We should not forget that an important part of the 1905 upheavals was the ethnic unrest in Poland, the Baltic region and the Trans-caucasus – after all only about 44 per cent of the population of the Russian Empire was Russian (see page 11). It has not been possible in a single chapter such as this to do these movements justice, but you should bear in mind that they are a significant dimension.

You might also wonder why so little attention has been paid to the revolutionaries – Lenin and the Bolsheviks, in particular. The simple answer to this is that they were not important. As we have indicated, the revolution was spontaneous and took the revolutionaries by surprise. The only figure to play a significant role in 1905 was the Menshevik, Leon Trotsky, who was briefly president of the St Petersburg Soviet. The Soviet proved to be a blueprint for worker organisation that could be revived during the next upheaval, in 1917. The Bolsheviks failed in their rising in Moscow in December 1905 and the revolutionary left in general underestimated the masses' wish to be represented in the Duma. Lenin is only important if we wish to read history backwards. Because he was important in 1917 does not mean to say he was important in 1905, though what he was doing is not without interest. He was not, however, relevant for the purpose of this chapter.

Essay writing

A few tips

The purpose of the essay question is to show that you have mastered the material on a particular topic and are able to support or refute arguments – your own as well as the historians you have read.

You must, above all, **address the question** – which can mean simply clarifying its meaning by defining key terms if there are ambiguities, or answering the question straight away if there are not.

The greatest enemy of the effective essay is irrelevance. Anything which interrupts the flow of your argument must be left out (remember you have limited time). However, facts and examples which are related to your argument are as important as the argument itself; those which are not are totally valueless. Do not think that if you simply put every detail down, they will make your case for you. They will not. This narrative approach will only achieve a low grade at best. You must learn to be analytical and refer to the question whenever it is appropriate. It cannot be emphasised too strongly that most A and AS Level casualties in history are those students who have not mastered relevance.

As far as style is concerned you should maintain the pressure of persuasion on the examiner by using short and concise sentences. Remember: ABC – accuracy, brevity and clarity – are the most important characteristics of style.

A suggested format

You should use the **introduction** to address the question, define its terms and in effect answer it by explaining your view. You should remember that examiners are marking hundreds of A- and AS-Level essays in a very short period of time and they want to know if you know the answer (there can be several 'right' ones but many more 'wrong' ones). They do not want to have to wade through pages of narrative until the question is finally addressed in the conclusion (*'thus in answer to the question we can see that . . .'*). You have to get the examiner on your side, right from the start.

If you adopt this approach, the rest of the essay will then justify the position you have taken at the beginning by developing the argument with factual support. By the time you reach the end your **conclusion** should be almost superfluous; you have answered the question and you should have the marks in the bag. You might wish to reiterate your argument or further impress the examiner by pointing forward or looking back, outside the confines of the question, in order to show the breadth of your knowledge.

An actual essay

How did the Tsar survive the 1905 Revolution?

By way of introduction you might wish to question the question by suggesting it was not a revolution, but this could be a semantic cul de sac. Far better would be a direct answer which might suggest three factors that enabled the Tsar to survive:

- The lack of coordination of his opponents (this is where you might question the epithet 'revolution')
- the making of timely concessions
- the use of force to repress unrest.

Each of your paragraphs would develop these points and you might wish to assess which is the most important of the three. By the time you reach your conclusion you should have answered the question, so you might want to point forward and suggest that although the Tsar had survived 1905, the grievances that emerged at that time had not been satisfied and would emerge again in 1917.

CHAPTER THREE

WAS THE TSARIST REGIME STABLE OR UNSTABLE IN 1914?

Objectives

◢ To establish whether the Tsarist regime was stable or unstable in 1914

◢ To decide whether the collapse of Tsarism was inevitable or imminent at that time.

The question above is an important historiographical one – that is to say it has generated much debate among historians. Fundamental to **Marxism** is the belief in historical inevitability, the belief that capitalism would collapse and inevitably lead to socialism. Soviet historians used to maintain that Russia was on the verge of revolution in 1914. Many other historians believe that the Russian regime was bound to collapse though they feel the war accelerated the process. Others believe that the regime was not on the verge of collapse in 1914. According to this view, the regime was relatively stable in 1914 and could have survived had it not been brought down by failure in the First World War. If we look at Russia in 1914 it might be possible to come to some conclusion about these various views.

KEY TERMS

Marxism is a philosophy of history and a programme of revolutionary reform expounded by Karl Marx (1818–83). Basically Marx believed that society would inevitably evolve through feudal, then capitalist, phases prior to achieving socialism, the highest form of human society. Feudalism was the medieval social system in which the majority of the population, usually peasants, worked the land for a few lords – the situation in Russia until 1861. According to Marx, capitalism would be overthrown as a result of class conflict: the **proletariat** (the industrial working class), exasperated at their exploitation by the rich factory owners, would rise in revolt and become the agents of revolution transforming capitalist society into a socialist one. Marx envisaged socialism as a world system – hence the expression 'world revolution' – in which nation states and even money would no longer exist. It was, however, a philosophy better understood by intellectuals than factory workers.

The peasantry

As we saw in the previous chapter, during the course of 1905 to 1907 there had been considerable peasant unrest aimed mainly at the noble landowners. Much of this had been put down by repression but the government also passed a number of measures designed to alleviate the situation, including the abolition of redemption dues and the extension of credit through the Peasant Land Bank.

When he became Prime Minister, Stolypin set himself the task of pacifying the peasantry as the key to Russia's long-term stability. Many of the measures passed had been discussed for some time but it was he who put them into practice; it is therefore appropriate to describe them as his measures. During the unrest the government had observed that the commune had not been a guarantee of rural stability – indeed it gave disturbances their cohesion and organisation. Therefore the solution was to encourage peasants to leave the commune and to become private landowners. Stolypin's policy was to create a group of peasant proprietors with a vested interest in maintaining the regime who would hold their revolutionary neighbours in check.

The reason Stolypin himself gave in the Duma for the agrarian reforms was his wish to create a class of small, independent farmers – a wager on 'the sober and strong' as he put it – who would be industrious and enterprising. It was felt that the existing system encouraged the increasing fragmentation of the land (because of the increase in population) and did not provide the incentive to make improvements (because the land did not remain in the family). In essence what Stolypin proposed was privatisation – and the consolidation of scattered strips. In August 1906 Stolypin made 6 million hectares of state and crown land available for peasant purchase and in October all restrictions on peasant movement were removed. However, the key measure was his **Land Law** of 9 November 1906. (This was passed by decree and was not approved by the Duma until June 1910.) It stated:

◢ Source

By Our Manifesto of 3 November 1905 redemption payments by peasants for allotment land were abolished as from 1 January 1907. From then on those lands will be free from any restrictions imposed on them because of this payment and peasants will be granted the right to leave the commune freely and individual households will be able to obtain part of the communal land stock as their own property ...

Whole communes, both those where land is held in communal tenure as well as those where it is held by individual tenure, may change to a system of consolidated holding for each peasant, by a two-thirds majority of peasants eligible to vote at the village meeting.

Martin McCauley, **Octobrists to Bolsheviks: Imperial Russia 1905–1917**
(Edward Arnold, 1984)

How successful was this reform? Historians are divided though most concede it was a good idea. Lenin himself stated: 'If Stolypin's agrarian policy was maintained for a very long period, and if it succeeded finally in transforming the whole structure of rural landholding ... it could make us abandon any attempt at an agrarian policy in a bourgeois society'. In truth, the effects were limited for a variety of reasons:

◢ Stolypin himself believed that the reforms would require 20 years to complete – in fact, it only operated for nine and after his death in 1911 it was not given the same priority.

◢ Most peasants were opposed to the legislation; they actually believed in the commune.

◢ Many peasants were reluctant to leave the commune for economic and social reasons – many felt a private farm might not be viable and many (justifiably) feared the hostility of those who remained in the commune.

Thus by 1916 just over 20 per cent of those who remained holding land by communal tenure had privatised but only about 10 per cent of all peasant landholdings were consolidated. Moreover, it tended to be the poorer peasants who bought the land, only to sell it; and consolidation was vehemently resisted by the commune.

The effect of the reform varied – it had some success in the South and West, but made little headway in central Russia.

Separations from the Communes

Year	Households
1907	48,271
1908	508,344
1909	579,409
1910	342,245
1911	145,567
1912	122,314
1913	134,554
1914	97,877
1915	29,851
Total	2,008,432

Thus it must be recognised that Stolypin's reform did not achieve the goals that he himself set. 'No "agrarian revolution" occurred and no Russian yeomanry emerged' (Richard Pipes). The time was too short, the numbers too few, the gains too far in the future to help the present.

The main problem remained land hunger caused by the rapidly increasing population. Indeed between 1900 and 1910 the population increased from 132.9 million to 160.7 million – an increase of 21 per cent, the fastest growth rate in Europe. Stolypin tried to ease this problem by continuing the policy of encouraging peasants to migrate to less densely populated areas such as Siberia. As the table opposite shows this had some success, but it only dealt with about 10 per cent of the population increase.

Given the fact that there was such pressure on the land, it is remarkable that there was not massive unrest in this period. There were two reasons for this. One was that Russian agriculture was becoming more efficient. As mentioned in Part One, new land, new crops and new rotations meant that crop yields went up by 50 per cent between 1861 and 1910. This helped to support the enormous growth in population. Secondly, there were a series of exceptional harvests from 1909 through to 1913. Thus it was a fact that the countryside was relatively quiet on the eve of the First World War and this clearly contributed to the stability of the regime.

On the other hand, it can be argued that these exceptional harvests merely masked peasant discontent which remained as intense as ever.

Migration to Siberia, 1905–13

Total migrants		Irregulars	Returners
1905	44,029	92.6	11,524
1906	216,648	50.8	46,262
1907	567,979	19.7	117,518
1908	758,812	47.7	121,204
1909	707,463	47.9	139,907
1910	353,000	(c. 20%)	(70,000)*
1911	226,100	–	(64,000)
1912	259,600	–	(34,000)
1913	327,900	–	(23,000)
	3,461,531		

*These figures are not complete

The peasants were now more assertive, more demanding; they had rising expectations. It is undoubtedly true that they continued to resent noble ownership and to call for its abolition. However, in truth noble ownership of land was neither as great as it had been nor, given the rapid growth of population, would its abolition have necessarily solved the problem of land hunger in the long term.

In 1861 the nobles had retained over a half of their land but many sold up as they could not make agriculture pay (civil service pay proved more lucrative for many). They sold up at a rate of about 1 per cent per annum so that by the turn of the century they had disposed of 40 per cent of their holdings. What had been a trickle became a flood after 1905 when a further 12 per cent of noble land was sold off. So it might appear that noble landownership was withering away. However, noble estates were not a myth, a small proportion of the people still owned a great deal of good land. Moreover, it was this land that the peasants wanted. Having said all that, the fact is that the countryside was quiet in 1914. Discontent may have not been far from the surface, Stolypin's reforms may have been faltering, and land hunger undoubtedly remained a problem, but as long as the village was quiet, the Tsar was safe from peasant revolution. In fact, for many peasants living conditions were actually improving.

The working class

The revolution of 1905 had made plain the potential power of the industrial labour force. But the crushing of the Moscow rising at the end of 1905 had had a demoralising effect and the workers took little part in the events of 1906. The number of strikes dropped dramatically, as the table below shows, so that industrial strife had almost ceased by 1909. Although workers had been given the right to form unions – 300,000 workers were in unions in 1907 – they were repeatedly closed down on technical grounds so that only about 40,000 were in unions in 1913. Clearly, faith in collective bargaining could not take root. Faith in political parties also declined; for instance, membership of the Social Democrats which had been as high as 150,000 in 1907, slumped to 10,000 in 1910. The truth is that the workers could not obtain representation through the ballot box. Many left-wing parties remained illegal and only 13 deputies out of a total of 413 served their interests in the Duma.

	Number of strikers
1905	2,863,173
1906	1,108,406
1907	740,074
1908	176,101
1909	64,166
1910	46,623
1911	105,110
1912	725,491
1913	887,096
1914 (first 6 months)	1,337,458

By 1908 Russian industry had recovered from the disorder of 1905–6. After 1910 it underwent an enormous (armaments-led) expansion. Industrial growth was 6 per cent per annum between 1907 and 1914. Needless to say this expansion led to a considerable increase in the workforce, up by fully one-third from 1910 to 1914. This put an enormous strain on public services, transport and housing. Industrial strife returned after February 1912 with the shooting of unarmed strikers in the **Lena Goldfields** (200 killed and about 400 wounded) and in the first six months of 1914 1.3 million workers downed tools.

Thus by 1914 the level of industrial unrest was comparable to that in 1905. In July the Bolsheviks attempted to exploit a great strike that brought St Petersburg to a standstill but other sections of society did not support it and the police (with army back-up) were able to restore order.

Low wages, long hours and poor housing remained significant grievances but protests became more political and workers did not distinguish between protest against their employers and protests against the government. The rapid influx of peasants into the Russian work-force seems to have increased its militancy, though it should be remembered that much of the Russian working class retained strong rural links. Many still had land and perhaps a wife in the village. However, it was in fact the most urbanised workers – those with the highest level of skills, education, and wages – who were at the fore-front of labour protest. It seems, then, that grievances were the product of class consciousness articulated by those who recognised the inherent indignity of the crude Russian factory system.

To sum up, the proletariat expanded significantly after 1910 and industrial unrest returned with a vengeance from 1912. However, there were no legal means of redress: 'just as the regime's handling of industrial relations precluded the emergence of a moderate trade union move-ment, so its political stance precluded the emergence of a reformist party' (Edward Acton). In the absence of a reformist path, revolution seemed the only alternative, but the July 1914 rising demonstrated that the regime could still rely on the loyalty of the army and the police, and the army could overcome striking workers. The Russian proletariat was not stable in 1914, it was seething with discontent, but the regime was still in control.

The middle class

The liberalisation of the political system – the wish of the middle class – might have offered the workers an alternative path, but this had not come about. The middle classes undoubtedly benefited from economic growth – individual wealth grew, from top industrialists down to the humble shopkeeper, and increasing numbers became middle class, as the demand for white-collar workers (clerks and managers) and pro-fessionals (lawyers, teachers, doctors) expanded. However, there was no equivalent increase in political influence. Indeed, the influence of the liberal parties was actually in decline.

The creation of the Duma, for all its limitations, established the idea of parliamentary government and provided a forum for debate. However, the landed nobility dominated the upper house (the State Council) and after the Electoral Reform of 1907 there was a large number of them in the Third and Fourth Dumas. They showed no inclination to cooperate with the middle class and blocked even Stolypin's moderate package of reforms. Hence constitutional government did not evolve. After Stolypin's assassination in 1911, the middle-class parties – the Octobrists, the Progressives and the Kadets – became more outspoken in their criticism of the government.

The middle classes were also deeply divided – economically, regionally, ethnically and culturally – but their real dilemma was their fear of the masses. They were unable to influence the government and unable (and unwilling) to appeal to the masses (for fear of social revolution).

The liberal predicament appeared to be insoluble as the liberals were caught between the intransigence of the Right and radicalism of the Left. The path of constitutional monarchy might yet have been the best option for the regime in the long term. However, far from embracing the educated classes, the regime positively alienated them – even moderate conservatives were exasperated by the Tsar's indifference, and the incompetence of the government. The middle classes were a potential source of support for the regime – but by 1914 they too were in opposition.

◢ Source

Whither is the government policy, or rather lack of policy, carrying us? Towards an inevitable and grave catastrophe! Never were those revolutionary organisations which aim at violent upheaval so broken and impotent as they are now, and never were the Russian public and the Russian people so profoundly revolutionised by the actions of the government, for day by day faith in the government is steadily waning, and with it is waning faith in the possibility of a peaceful issue from the crisis.

*Alexander Guchkov, leader of the Octobrists, in November 1913; quoted in Martin McCauley, **Octobrists to Bolsheviks: Imperial Russia 1905–1917** (Edward Arnold, 1984)*

It is ironic in fact that on the eve of the First World War the revolutionaries believed the regime to be secure and never felt more pessimism, while its potential supporters also felt pessimism but for the opposite reason; they felt collapse was imminent.

The government

Was the government as incompetent as Guchkov suggested? Was it on its last legs in 1914? If we simply look at the economy and measure it by present day concerns – balance of payments, a balanced budget, industrial growth – then Imperial Russia was in very good shape indeed.

Basic statistics

	1900	1910	1913
Population (millions)	132.9	160.7	175.1 (1914)
Pig iron production (m. poods)	179.1	185.8	283.0
Coal production (m. poods)	986.3	1,526.3	2,200.1
Railways ('000 km end yr)	53.2	66.6	70.2
Consumption of cotton (m. poods)	16.0	22.1	25.7
Imports (m. roubles)	626.3	1,084.4	(1,084.4)
Exports (m. roubles)	716.2	1,449.0	1,520.0
Budget revenue (ordinary,m. roubles)	1,704.1	2,780.9	3,417.3
Budget expenditure (ordinary,m. roubles)	1,599.1	2,473.1	3,094.2

From these statistics we can see that industrial growth was up, the value of exports exceeded imports and government revenue exceeded expenditure. In addition, there was a considerable growth in both savings and savings accounts, gold reserves increased, the national debt was coming down and the government was becoming less reliant on foreign loans. However, the vast majority of the people did not derive much benefit from these favourable economic circumstances.

What of the government's political performance? Most historians are agreed that Stolypin was a fine Prime Minister. We have already observed that his policies combined repression with reform. The centrepiece of his reforms was the land law, but this did not achieve what was expected of it. Stolypin changed the electoral law so that he could work with the Duma; he hoped that a cooperative approach between the government and representatives of the educated elite would strengthen the State's authority and reduce social tension. Yet Stolypin was only able to enact a fraction of his legislation. Measures to increase religious toleration, reduce discrimination against the Jews, extend primary education, discipline local officials, extend peasant representation in the *zemstva* and establish a new, lower-level tier of *zemstva* on an all-class franchise all met with problems. Not only were many of his proposals radically altered by the Duma, but he encountered stiff opposition from the State Council and the Tsar himself only gave lukewarm support.

His difficulties were epitomised by his 1911 bill to establish *zemstva* in the western provinces (*i.e.* Poland) which was rejected by the State Council with the Tsar's consent. On this issue Stolypin's frustration was intense. He threatened resignation unless the Tsar promulgated the law by decree (Article 87). The Tsar consented but felt humiliated, the State Council was furious and the Duma denounced his unconstitutional behaviour. Stolypin succeeded but had alienated everyone in the process. Although he had the best intentions he was, as a contemporary put it, politically dead some time before his actual death by assassination in October 1911. In truth Stolypin, despite his sense of purpose, achieved very little; but if a man of his stature could achieve very little then what hope was there for the regime? Stolypin was undermined by the very people he was trying to save. Though often disliked, contemporaries respected Stolypin's intelligence; they had little respect for his successors.

Stolypin's successors were chosen because they were unlikely to have a programme of their own: they would be malleable, they would be loyal. His immediate successor was Vladimir Kokovstov, a clever man who had been an efficient Minister of Finance for the past six years or so. However, Kokovstov lacked charisma and had little influence with either the other ministers or the Duma (this suited the Tsar). Accordingly he did not work with the Duma, believing that sound economy rather than reform was all that Russia needed. He seemed to believe that there was little discontent within Russia; it existed only within the Duma. Needless to say the Duma did become more troublesome in the face of the government's disregard, but the Prime Minister felt he could ignore it secure in the knowledge that the deputies – men of property and privilege – would not lead an assault on the regime. Kokovstov was himself replaced at the beginning of 1914 by Ivan Goremykin, a 74-year-old who did not want the appointment. He was not expected to do anything; the idea was to undermine the power of the Prime Minister. This Nicholas also did by ensuring that Goremykin only held one portfolio – his predecessors had held two. The weakening of the role of the Prime Minister only led to growing governmental paralysis.

Thus cooperation with the Duma virtually ceased and the Prime Minister was a pawn. If we consider this together with the Lena Gold-fields massacre, the Beilis case (a scandalous judicial prosecution that highlighted the antisemitism of the regime) and the rise of Gregori Rasputin (an illiterate peasant who seemed to have inordinate influence over the royal couple – of whom more later), we can understand why the Moscow manufacturer P. P. Riabushinski exclaimed before a congress of industrialists in May 1914, 'our government is not talented. If this goes on, even the broad masses will lose respect for authority . . . One can only hope our great country will outlive its petty government.' The basis of the regime's support was becoming narrower all the time. Who was responsible for this state of affairs? Just one man, the Tsar.

Tsar Nicholas II

What options were open to the Tsar? He could embrace reform, take the liberal path and avert revolution. This he was not prepared to do. Indeed Nicholas himself wished to water down the constitution still further in 1913 but even the arch-conservative President of the State Council told him he had created the system and would have to live with it. Alternatively, he could uphold the *status quo* – the option he came to favour – but to do this the Tsar needed to be a resolute and impressive personality, which Nicholas was not. His lack of charisma and poor judgement of people created disquiet even within the establishment. The royal couple were unpopular at Court and inspired little loyalty even among those whose respect for the throne was greatest. In addition, the establishment itself was weakening – the influence of the Church was in decline, and the numbers of landed aristocracy reducing. There was even a question mark hanging over the army. The mutinies of 1905–6 had shown that shorter periods of service might have contributed to a less reliable force. Imperial Russia needed a tsar with vision who could adapt the regime to meet the challenges thrown up by rapid change and who could reduce the levels of discontent throughout society. Nicholas II was not that man.

Conclusion

So what can we say in conclusion? Even though the countryside was quiet, the peasants were eager to seize the nobles' estates; in the factories there was considerable industrial unrest, with strike levels rising; and the middle classes were frustrated by the failure of the constitutional experiment. After Stolypin, the government itself lacked direction as Tsar Nicholas sought to undermine the position of Prime Minister. The overwhelming impression one is left with is that Russian society was seething with discontent and the Tsarist government was incompetent and unpopular. But is it that simple?

The trends were contradictory and one can make a case for the opposite view. Stolypin's repression, accompanied by economic prosperity, had succeeded in restoring order. The regime had weathered the Revolution of 1905 and its opponents were pessimistic. The countryside was quiet, the peasantry was not in revolt; successive good harvests had brought better times. The economy as a whole was performing well and the middle classes were benefiting. The constitutional experiment was not a complete disaster; there was full support for the government's rearmament programme in the Duma, and some useful legislation was passed: the law of 1908 had eventually led to a considerable expansion of primary school education, and in 1912 elected justices of the peace were restored, land captains' powers reduced and workers' insurance was introduced. In any event the liberals were on the defensive and were unlikely to ally with the masses again as they had done in 1905. They feared social revolution. They were unlikely to bring the regime down.

Clearly there was considerable industrial unrest but it was mainly confined to the capital and the government had little trouble containing it. Indeed in 1914 the troops were not needed as the strike collapsed before they arrived and the police could cope. 'In fact the chances of revolution in 1914 were very slim' (Lieven). The situation was nowhere near as bad as 1905 *and the Tsar had survived that.* The army appeared to be loyal and as long as Nicholas could rely on the bureaucracy, the police and the army, his position was secure. After all there have been many examples of unpopular regimes lasting a long time. As we noticed when looking at 1905, there would need to be co-ordinated opposition and a viable alternative to the Tsarist regime, as well as a breakdown of military loyalty, in order to remove the Tsar – and that combination was rather unlikely in 1914. But if the regime was not on the verge of collapse in 1914, it is also true to say that it could not go on forever with such a narrow basis of support. Any crisis could unleash the various discontents in Russian society and lead to revolution. The regime had to evolve but with Nicholas II at the helm this was only likely to occur under duress.

Russia then was a mixture of stability and instability in 1914 but the collapse of Tsarism was neither inevitable nor necessarily imminent. However, the decision to go to war in 1914 proved fatal. It created the crisis that brought the monarchy down. Given the fact that both the Crimean and Russo–Japanese Wars had created crises that shook the monarchy, it is quite remarkable that the government should have gone to war in 1914 at all. To this decision we now turn.

Documentary sources

The format

Documentary sources at A and AS Level tend to be contemporary sources and the object of the exercise is, usually, to test **recall**, **comprehension**, **comparison** and **evaluation**.

Thus an initial question might simply use the source as a prompt to test **recall** (*i.e.* memory/knowledge) by, for instance, referring to a historical figure in the source and asking his position in government. A second question might ask you to explain a source (*i.e.* **comprehension**) by expressing its content in a succinct and simplified way, or it might require you to **evaluate** its usefulness. This would require you to analyse the content and possibly determine whether or not it is reliable – though even unreliable sources can be useful if you are aware of their unreliability (*i.e.* propaganda may give a false message but at least it tells you what false message someone is trying to get across). However, do not fall into the trap of giving a stock answer *e.g.* 'but this document might be biased' when you do not really know whether or not it is. You might be missing the point: many documents used in these exercises are reliable and you can take them at face value. The art of doing well is knowing what you can and cannot trust.

Yet another question might require you to **compare** two or three sources to determine which is/are more useful, or how it might be possible to reconcile or explain seemingly contradictory statements. Again an evaluation of the content is necessary and an assessment of reliability is sometimes (but not always) necessary – as indeed is your knowledge of the topic. Sometimes it is appropriate to inject your own knowledge or refer to another document. A final question usually asks a general question which you have to answer by referring to all the sources (and you should always do this by referring to all the sources *by letter throughout*) and by employing your own knowledge.

Of course documentary exercises vary considerably both in terms of the number and types of sources and in terms of the questions asked, but recall, comprehension, comparison and evaluation will probably be common to them all.

Exercise

Take Stolypin's Land Law on page 54 as document A and Separation from the Communes on page 56 as document B and then answer the following questions:

a   i   In document A explain the references to 'redemption payments' and 'the commune'   *4 marks*

    ii   `What benefits was it hoped 'consolidated holdings' would bring?

           4 marks

b   Look at document B. Why was there (i) such a marked rise in the number of households finally leaving the communes between 1907 and 1909, and (ii) such a marked fall in the number of households leaving between 1913 and 1915?   *8 marks*

c   Who gained and who lost as a result of Stolypin's Land Law of 9 November 1906?   *8 marks*

d   Why did Bolsheviks, Octobrists and Kadets respond differently to Stolypin's land reform programme?   *9 marks**

*You will need to look beyond this book for the answer to this one.

Oxford and Cambridge Examination Board (1990)

CHAPTER FOUR

WHY WAS NICHOLAS II FORCED TO ABDICATE IN 1917?

Objectives

◢ To determine the causes of the abdication

◢ To analyse why the Revolution happened when it did.

Russia was not ready for war in 1914 yet Nicholas felt unable to resist some gesture of support for Serbia. Once the war had begun, defeat brought the regime to the verge of collapse, though this took over two years. By 1917 the government and the Tsar, in particular, were completely discredited; the generals asked for Nicholas's abdication to avoid a revolution, but the belief that things would get better once he had gone proved illusory. He was swept away by defeat (as indeed the Habsburgs and Hohenzollerns were to be the following year) but there was no satisfactory alternative to put in his place.

Russian foreign policy 1905–14

The prestige of the dynasty was very much bound up with maintaining Russia's status as a great power. Consequently, defeat at the hands of the Japanese in 1904–5 proved to be a considerable humiliation not only for Russia but for the monarchy itself. In the aftermath of defeat, Russia was weak and the foreign secretary, Izvolski, tried to remain on good terms with all the powers. However, in the increasingly competitive and polarised world of the early twentieth century, this proved to be an impossible task. An agreement with Great Britain in 1907 which sought, among other things, to resolve spheres of influence in Persia reinforced ties with Paris as Britain and France were drawing closer together. On the other hand, Izovski's attempts in 1908 to reach an agreement with Austria proved disastrous.

The so-called **Bosnian Crisis of 1908–9** originated in Austria's determination to annex Bosnia outright. Izvolski attempted to arrange a tit-for-tat agreement whereby Russia would secretly approve the annexation in return for Austrian support for the free passage of

Russian warships through the Straits of the Bosphorus, from the Black Sea to the Sea of Marmora and into the Mediterranean (see Figure 5 overleaf). Britain and France were not enthusiastic about Russia's wish for free passage. Despite this, Austria went ahead and annexed Bosnia claiming full Russian support. Stolypin, the Duma and the Russian press were appalled at this betrayal of fellow Slavs. But worse was to come; in 1909 Vienna demanded Russia's formal recognition of the annexation and Germany sent an ultimatum demanding immediate and unconditional compliance. Russia was too weak to do anything other than agree: its humiliation was complete. Nicholas was furious; Izvolski was eventually removed.

This crisis proved to be a significant turning-point in Russian foreign policy. Russia was determined not to be humiliated again, and stepped up its rearmament programme. There was to be no *rapprochement* with Austria; indeed Russian strategy was now to build up its influence in the Balkans to thwart Austrian expansion. At the same time, attempts were made to keep on reasonable terms with the Germans who could restrain the Austrians – but clearly Russia's true friends were France and Britain.

However, any policy that sought to control events in the Balkans was also bound to fail. Italian success against the Ottoman Turkish Empire in 1911 proved to be a green light for the aspirations of the Balkan states and in two Balkan Wars (1912 and 1913), the Turks were almost pushed out of Europe. The failure of Russia to either control or benefit from these developments was a matter of concern in St Petersburg but in truth the real loser was not Russia but Austria. Serbia had doubled in size and now, according to Vienna, constituted a real threat to the integrity of the Habsburgs' multi-ethnic empire. Austria now resolved to do something about Serbia – but Serbia was Russia's major ally in the Balkans. A crisis was brewing though Nicholas did not appear to see it coming; he remained optimistic that these complex matters could be resolved by negotiation and agreement.

Peter Durnovo, the former Minister of the Interior and a member of the State Council, was not so optimistic. In a memorandum he wrote in February 1914, he stated:

Figure 5 The growth of Balkan independence, 1822–1913. The dates refer to the year in which independence was gained from Turkey.

◢ Source

For there can be no doubt that . . . war will necessitate expenditures which are beyond Russia's limited financial means . . . a general European war is mortally dangerous both for Russia and Germany no matter who wins. It is our firm conviction . . . that there must inevitably break out in the defeated country a social revolution which, by the very nature of things, will spread . . .

*Martin McCauley, **Octobrists to Bolsheviks: Imperial Russia 1905–1917***
(Edward Arnold, 1984)

Durnovo was actually arguing for good relations between Russia and Germany as the bulwarks of conservatism. In fact, on the surface, relations between Russia and Germany were quite good though Germany's role in reforming the Turkish army was a source of some concern. Of greater concern in Berlin, however, was Russia's **Great Military Programme** announced in 1912, initiated in 1914 and due for completion in 1917. Though this programme remained largely on paper, it envisaged significant improvements in the railway network and administrative procedures which would enable the Russians to mobilise in 18 days. This alarmed the German High Command as it would render their Schlieffen Plan inoperable. This plan, originally drawn up from 1895 but subsequently amended, had become something of a holy writ in German strategic thinking. It was devised to fight a war on two fronts after the formation of the Franco–Russian alliance (1892/4); it envisaged a massive attack on France which would knock it out in six weeks (as in 1870), followed by the transfer of the army to the eastern front to deal with the Russians who would take that time to mobilise. The Russian programme created enormous pessimism among the German High Command and Moltke, the Chief of Staff, was heard to recommend a war 'sooner rather than later' while Germany could win. Indeed Germany's fear of Russia's potential military might may well have been the fundamental cause of the First World War; but of course it was the assassination in Sarajevo that provided the spark.

The outbreak of war

The Austrian Archduke, Franz Ferdinand, was assassinated by Serb terrorists in Sarajevo on 28 June 1914. After that, events moved rather slowly although the Germans did give Vienna the so-called 'blank cheque' (a promise of full support) on 5 July. The Austrians finally sent their ultimatum to Serbia on 23 July. When Sazonov, the Russian foreign minister, saw the text, he exclaimed: 'This means war in Europe!' He informed the Tsar that the ultimatum was impossible to accept and probably concocted with connivance from Berlin (he was right on both counts). He also maintained that the Central Powers were starting a war now because they believed they could win it. Nicholas, however, felt Sazonov was panicking and remained oblivious to the seriousness of the situation. Indeed as Europe stood on the brink of catastrophe his diary makes it clear that the Tsar still found time to fill his life with trivia – playing tennis, going for walks with his family and visiting relatives for tea. Finally on 28 July, Nicholas responded to his ministers' argument that Russia could not stand idly by and let Austria swallow Serbia; he agreed to a partial mobilisation of the army. This was meant to be a warning to Austria, but Vienna declared war on Serbia the same day. Now Nicholas hesitated. Two days later, after pressure from his military advisers, he agreed on full mobilisation. This set off alarm bells in Berlin and on 31 July the Germans demanded a halt, but Nicholas did not respond. On 1 August Germany declared war on Russia, and proceeded to put the Schlieffen Plan into operation. The First World War had begun.

Lenin had commented in 1913 that a war in Europe would be a very useful thing for the revolution 'but it is hardly possible that Franz Josef and Nicky would give us this pleasure'. Nicholas II did not want war in 1914; Russia was not ready, and would not be so until the completion of the military programme in 1917. However, many felt Russia's status as a great power was at stake. It is important to remember that the aristocratic sense of honour which had for so long been settled by the duel, made prestige and status inordinately important to the decision-makers of 1914. After the humiliations of 1904–5 and 1908–9 Russia could not afford to abandon its fellow Slavs in Serbia. But Russia did not declare war and many in the upper echelons of society had no illusions about the risks involved. On announcing the news, Nicholas himself was pale and gaunt, and the Empress burst into tears.

Nicholas appears to have been swept along by events almost against his will, and it is characteristic of him that he should order a partial mobilisation and only later discover that this was not feasible. Could war have been avoided? Of course it could, but if we accept that Germany was determined to force a war, then the Russian government did not have much room for manoeuvre in this crisis.

The war

In Russia and elsewhere across Europe, the declaration of war was greeted with a surge of patriotic enthusiasm. Huge crowds gathered at the Winter Palace in St Petersburg and sang hymns; the crowds were even larger in Moscow. The Duma politicians united in unconditional support for the war effort. Strikes almost ceased and mobilisation went smoothly. All were united in the desire to beat the Germans, and with British and French help this was thought to be possible. Moreover, most thought the war would be short – Peter Durnovo was unusual in arguing that the war could prove lengthy and disastrous. Germany's failure to achieve a rapid victory over France in the West ensured that he would be right.

The first year, 1914–15

Enthusiasm for the war lasted about six months or so. Initially, the Imperial army – the 'Russian steamroller' as it was known in the West – moved swiftly into East Prussia but soon suffered large-scale defeats at Tannenberg and the Masurian Lakes. However, these were offset by success against the Austrians in Galicia, which was overrun. At the end of 1914 honours were even, but the extent of Russian casualties was considerable and the shortage of munitions showed up the inadequacies of the war effort. Six and a half million men had been mobilised by November, but they were issued with only 4.6 million rifles. The front stabilised until the spring of 1915.

If the first six months of the war had been barely satisfactory, then the next six were disastrous. A combined Austro-German offensive pushed the Russians out of Galicia and a major German attack along the rest of the line pushed them back 200–300 miles, with the loss of Poland, Lithuania and even parts of the Ukraine. After a year, Russian casualties were approaching a staggering 4 million killed, wounded, captured or missing; and it was little comfort that the Germans had failed to achieve their objectives (they had committed two-thirds of their army to this offensive in the hope of inflicting a decisive defeat). Polivanov, the Minister for War, perceptively observed that 'one should not forget that the army now is quite different from the one which marched forth at the beginning of the war'. Most of the officers were dead, as were the infantry and reserves: the army was no longer the loyal one of 1914.

The mood which had been enthusiastic at the beginning of the war changed drastically by the spring. All the belligerents faced munitions crises but in Russia the lack of shells and rifles created a political crisis fuelled by critical press reports and personal jealousies. The government was charged with incompetence and anyone with any responsibility usually blamed somebody else. In no other country was the war effort so undermined internally. 'By June 1915, the spirit of common purpose that had united the government and opposition . . . vanished, yielding to recriminations and hostility even more intense than the mood of 1904–5' (Richard Pipes). However, criticism in 1915 was mainly confined to the middle classes who had, in their turn, been the most enthusiastic group for the war in the first place.

Nicholas responded with a ministerial shake-up in June. In addition, the Tsar conceded the principle of cooperation, with the establishment of joint boards – committees consisting of government officials, private businessmen and Duma deputies – to deal with military shortages. The significance of these organisations was more political than economic. They were seen as a sort of parallel bureaucracy and were considered to be more efficient than the government one.

Although the important principle of cooperation with the educated elite was conceded with regard to the war effort, Nicholas would not make comparable political concessions. Indeed at this time of crisis he made two significant decisions that were to have a detrimental effect in the long-term:

◢ he decided to become Commander-in-Chief of the armed forces at the front;
◢ he rejected the overtures of the 'Progressive Bloc' to form a Duma-based cabinet.

Nicholas as Commander-in-Chief

There were good reasons why Nicholas should take over as Commander-in-Chief. The incumbent, the Grand Duke Nicholas, was in a state of panic and his generals were incompetent; the Tsar would be a more calming influence and his Chief-of-Staff, General Alekseev, who would decide strategy and operations, had some ability. In addition, many peasant soldiers still venerated their Tsar and there was some hope that morale would improve. Another consideration was that it prevented the military from colluding with the opposition at Nicholas's expense. Nicholas himself saw it as a necessary act of duty and patriotism. He left for the front on 22 August.

On the other hand, the Council of Ministers were horrified. They felt Nicholas would be held responsible for every reverse; but as it happened the front stabilised in the autumn as the Germans ran out of steam. However, the absence of the Tsar from the home front did have unfortunate consequences in the capital where the unpopular Tsarina, Alexandra, interfered with government, often at the behest of Rasputin. In addition, the opportunity to create a broad-based government was missed.

The 'Progressive Bloc' came into being in the summer of 1915 and consisted of two-thirds of the Duma and a sizeable proportion of the State Council (it thus represented conservatives as well as liberals). It had the support of some government ministers, much of the press and two important organisations – the Town Union and the *Zemstvo* Union – that had been created in August 1914 to help the war effort. The Bloc also appeared to have middle-class support in Moscow and the provinces. It concocted a legislative programme (presented on 25 August) but the details are unimportant; what is important is the fact that it was an attempt to create a partnership in government with wide support, an attempt to create a 'National Government' – a ministry of public confidence. On 21 August most ministers requested that Nicholas let the Duma form a government. Nicholas was unmoved; he was determined not to make the mistake he believed he had made in October 1905. He would not surrender any power, he would not compromise. Indeed he even decided to prorogue the Duma (which he did on 3 September). His response was greeted with disbelief. It isolated him from virtually all the educated classes. To ignore even conservatives was indeed short-sighted. But there was little the politicians could do; they did not want a revolution. However, as the front stabilised, the crisis abated. In the nine months that followed, Nicholas's firmness seemed to be vindicated.

1916

In the second year of the war the Russian army recovered. As we have stated, the front stabilised and the Germans decided to suspend offensive operations in the East. Thanks to greater cooperation between industry and government, and imports, the shortages of shells and rifles were finally overcome. When the 1916 campaigning season began, the Russian army was in fact larger and better equipped than at any previous time in the war. Indeed by the summer, the Imperial army was in a position to launch a major offensive. Prior to that, at the beginning of the year, it had enjoyed quite a bit of success on the Caucasian front against the Turks.

The Brusilov Offensive – named after the general who led it – brought the Austrian army to the verge of collapse in the summer. The Russian advance continued for 10 weeks on a front 200 miles long and Austrian losses may have been nearly a million (300,000 prisoners were taken). Once again Austria was saved by the Germans who transferred 15 divisions from the West. From here on the Austrians ceased to function independently but the Russians could not get the better of the Germans. Brusilov's success inspired the Romanians to join the war on the Allied side but they were soon overrun and their participation only succeeded in extending Russia's front line to the Black Sea. Despite suffering half a million casualties in this offensive, Russia's military performance in 1916 was quite encouraging.

The home front

Just as the front line was at its strongest, the home front began to crack. Whereas in 1915 it had been the educated classes which had become disaffected, in 1916 they were joined by all urban dwellers, but particularly the proletariat. The causes were primarily economic – shortage of food and fuel, and high prices – but the fusion of urban mass discontent with that of the liberal politicians (as in October 1905), proved to be a dangerous political cocktail. It completely unnerved many members of the establishment who now came to so fear revolution that they too demanded political change – and when that was not forthcoming, came to consider the removal of the Tsar himself.

Inflation was not initially a problem in Russia but prices began to rise at the end of 1915 and then more than doubled in 1916. This benefited the peasantry who could command high prices for their grain and high wages for labour (which was scarce because of conscription). In the autumn of 1916 the Department of Police reported that rural areas were 'contented and calm'. A succession of good harvests also meant there was plenty of surplus grain to sell. The situation in the cities, however, was not good, and inflation and shortages of food and fuel became acute in 1916. The urban population is estimated to have grown from 22 million to 28 million between 1914 and 1916, another colossal increase comparable to that which occurred after 1910. Wages could not keep pace with prices; in October 1916 the Police estimated that wages had risen 100 per cent in the past two years, but prices had gone up by 300 per cent. Everyone was affected – industrial workers, white-collar workers, government bureaucrats, and even the police themselves. The Department of Police warned that great danger existed of a popular explosion brought on by collapsing living standards. 'The ordinary inhabitant [is] condemned to a half-starved existence.' The head of police added that the government, including the Emperor himself, was held to blame. Indeed it was reported at the end of September 1916 that disaffection among the masses was now at a level comparable with that of 1905 (though the number of workers on strike was much less). Most observers agreed that a crisis was looming. What were the reasons for this crisis? There were three:

◢ the collapse of the rail network
◢ the requirements of the army
◢ the hoarding of grain by the peasants.

There was no shortage of grain, it was simply not getting to the towns. The rail network was in a state of serious deterioration (it had not been very good to begin with), the rolling stock was worn out, repairs were not being made, and the same applied to the railroad itself which was often single track. The retreat had also led to the loss of one of the two main north–south lines. The army had requisitioned about one-third of the rolling stock to transport soldiers and supplies including vast shipments of foodstuffs. The peasants began hoarding grain when it got to the point that there was nothing to buy (or what there was, was too expensive); there was no incentive to sell if there were no farming tools or consumer goods available. These were not being made as industry was concentrating on armament production.

The Tsar was aware of the crisis on the home front but bewildered as to how to resolve it. He had become, by the autumn of 1916, a shadow of his former self (which many would say was not much).

◢ Source

His Majesty is a changed man ... He is no longer seriously interested in anything. Of late, he has become quite apathetic. He goes through his daily routine like an automaton, paying more attention to the hour set for his meals or his walk in the garden, than to affairs of state. One can't rule an empire and command an army in the field in this manner. If he doesn't realise it in time, something catastrophic is bound to happen.

Paul Benckendorff, the Grand Marshal of the Court; quoted in Dominic Lieven,
Nicholas II *(John Murray, 1993)*

Back in Petrograd (as St Petersburg was renamed at the beginning of the war), the Tsar's absence left a great deal of power in the hands of the Tsarina Alexandra. Because she was German she was an easy target for rumours of treachery. She knew little about policies (Benckendorff described her as having 'a will of iron linked to not much brain') and concentrated more on personalities. Alexandra was also influenced by Rasputin, who only now began to have some say in appointments and policies, a factor which became well known in Petrograd. Regardless of his actual influence, popular perception believed it to be considerable; the fact that the Imperial couple could be swayed by an ignorant, debauched peasant did little for the monarchy's prestige. Alexandra encouraged Nicholas to change ministers with such frequency that the process became known as 'ministerial leapfrog'. Anyone who showed some independence of mind was replaced by someone whom the Empress and Rasputin liked – someone who would be loyal, obedient and unquestioning. These changes not only weakened the government but administrative continuity as well (in fact between August 1915 and February 1917 13 major ministries saw 36 ministers come and go). Together with the Tsar's apathy, all this meant that the civilian government was in many ways leaderless, in a state of drift. A vacuum was developing.

In the winter of 1916–17 enormous pressure built up on Nicholas II to concede a government which would be chosen from the Duma. When in September 1916 Nicholas had appointed the deputy chairman of the Duma, Alexander Protopopov, as Minister of the Interior, it aroused great hopes of a responsible ministry, but it was not to be. In fact, Protopopov turned out to be something of a disaster and seriously undermined the effectiveness of a crucial ministry at a critical time. At the beginning of November, Miliukov, the Kadet leader, made an inflammatory speech in the Duma in which he attacked the government for its incompetence and ended by wondering whether it was the result of stupidity or perhaps even treason.

Conservatives, and even members of the royal family, now warned Nicholas of impending revolution and begged him to make concessions.

◢ Source

Literally everyone is worried ... about Russia's internal condition. They say straight out that if matters go on as now within Russia we will never succeed in winning the war ... the universal cry is for ... the establishing of a responsible ministry. This measure is considered to be the only one which could avoid a general catastrophe.

> The Grand Duke George writing in November 1916; quoted in
> Dominic Lieven, **Nicholas II** (John Murray, 1993)

Nicholas did not respond. Many now came to see him as an obstacle to victory and a guarantee of revolution. For the first time liberals and monarchists made common cause against the crown. The oppositional mood even spread to the generals – General Krymov told Rodzianko, the chairman of the Duma, that the army would welcome a *coup d'état*. Even the murder of Rasputin in December – undertaken by members of the aristocracy in a desperate attempt to reduce the damage being inflicted on the monarchy – could not reverse the Tsar's growing isolation. Although Nicholas appeared to no longer have the will to stand firm, he still failed to respond constructively to any suggestions. As 1916 drew to a close, the political situation was serious. The extreme left wanted a revolution; the liberals wanted constitutional government and many on the right simply wished to replace Nicholas. Indeed a number of conspiracies were afoot to that end but they were not successful at this time. The Tsar himself was exhausted and depressed, a man out of his depth.

The February Revolution

Even before the war the cities of the north – Petrograd and Moscow – were dependent on the grain-producing regions of the south. During the war, as we have already indicated, the pattern of supply had broken down as the rail network became increasingly disrupted. By late 1916 the two cities were only getting about one-third of their food requirements; and Petrograd only about half the fuel it needed. After two mild winters, 1916–17 proved to be bitterly cold so the fuel shortage became even more serious – factories had to be shut, and bakeries could not bake. Moreover, freezing weather also immobilised much rolling stock (about 60,000 trucks) and heavy snow blocked lines. Army rations had to be reduced as well.

However, despite all this hardship and the anxiety of the middle class, the workers endured these deterioratiang conditions with remarkable restraint. No one was actually starving, and industrial unrest was not yet serious. Despite police comparisons, the level of strikes in 1916 was running at less than a quarter of that of 1905 (and the demands were economic rather than political). The panic developing in the elite was not based on what was happening, but what might happen.

On 9 January 1917 the Workers' Group (of the War Industries Committee) in Petrograd issued a strike call for the anniversary of Bloody Sunday and 140,000 workers responded. Next the group planned a demonstration on 14 February when the Duma was due to reconvene, to call for a radical change in government. Protopopov moved to prevent this by arresting the Workers' Group leadership on 27 January and placing military control of the city under the Cossack General Khabalov. This had the desired effect; the demonstration was called off, but even so 90,000 workers went on strike that day. The strike movement was now gaining a momentum of its own, though demonstrations remained peaceful for the time being and the cold weather kept many indoors. However on 21 February the Putilov Works had to shut down because of lack of fuel and tens of thousands of workers were laid off. The next day the Tsar, who had returned to Petrograd for Christmas, decided to return to the front. Suddenly, to everyone's surprise, the situation transformed dramatically; disorders broke out that would not subside, aided perhaps by a short period of mild weather.

On International Women's Day (23 February) a procession of demonstrating women, protesting against the shortages of bread and the long queues, coalesced with about 100,000 workers on strike or locked out. On 24 February, 200,000 workers came out on the streets and the following day the numbers rose as high as 300,000. It was becoming clear that the workers were determined to sustain the protest. Nicholas, unaware of the seriousness of the situation, demanded that order be restored by military force. On 26 February, military units took up positions around the city and in several districts the troops opened fire. By nightfall order seemed to have been restored though ominously a small mutiny had occurred among some of the garrison troops but it had been contained. On the same day, Nicholas ordered that the Duma be prorogued.

Then on **27 February**, all hell broke loose. The garrison mutinied and the mutinous soldiers fraternised with the the striking workers. Prisoners were released from the Peter and Paul Fortress, the Ministry of the Interior was sacked, the Okhrana headquarters overrun and the Winter Palace occupied. Shops, restaurants and private houses were looted and arsenals rifled. Of the 160,000-strong garrison, half was in full mutiny and the rest simply looked on. The authorities were helpless. The ministers asked to resign so they could make way for a Duma ministry. Nicholas refused their request and decided to return to Petrograd himself. He called upon his generals to assemble reliable troops to put down the mutiny. At this stage only Petrograd was in revolt; the rest of the country was quiet. On 28 February General Chief of Staff Alekseev reported these events to his generals:

◢ Source

On 27 February about midday, the President of the State Duma reported that the troops were going over to the side of the population and killing their officers. General Khabalov around midday on the 27th reported to His Majesty that one company of the Pavlovsky Regiment's reserve battalion had declared on 26 February that it would not fire on the people. The Commander of a battalion of this regiment was wounded by the crowd. On 27 February training detachments of the Volynsky Regiment refused to proceed against the rebels, and its commander shot himself. Then this detachment together with a company of the same regiment proceeded to the quarters of other reserve battalions, and men from these units began to join them . . .

On the 27th, after 7 p.m., the Minister of War reported that the situation in Petrograd had become very serious. The few units which have remained faithful to their duty cannot suppress the rebellion, and troop units have gradually joined the rebels. Fires have started. Petrograd has been placed under martial law . . .

On 28 February at 1 a.m. His Majesty received a telegram from General Khabalov stating that he could not restore order in the capital. The majority of the units have betrayed their duty and many have passed over to the side of the rebels. The troops which have remained faithful to their duty, after fighting the whole day, have suffered many casualties.

Towards evening the rebels seized the greater part of the capital, and the small units, which have remained faithful to their oath, have been rallied in the vicinity of the Winter Palace . . . At 2 a.m. the Minister of War reported that the rebels had occupied the Mariinsky palace and that the members of the revolutionary government were there . . . At 8.25., General Khabalov reported that the number of those who had remained faithful had dropped to 600 infantrymen and 500 cavalrymen with 15 machine guns and 12 guns having only 80 cartridges and that the situation was extremely difficult . . .

We have just received a telegram from the Minister of War, stating that the rebels have seized the most important buildings in all parts of the city. Due to fatigue and propaganda the troops have laid down their arms, passed to the side of the rebels, or become neutral. In the streets disorderly shooting is going on all the time; all traffic has stopped; officers and soldiers who appear in the streets are being disarmed.

The ministers are all safe, but apparently the work of the Ministry has stopped.

According to private information, the President of the State Council, Shcheglovitov, has been arrested. In the State Duma, a council of party leaders has been formed to establish contact for the revolutionary government with institutions and individuals. Supplementary elections to the Petrograd Soviet of Workers' and Soldiers' Deputies from the workers and the rebel troops have been announced.

We have just received a telegram from General Khabalov which shows that actually he cannot any longer influence events. Communicating to you the foregoing, I should add that we, the active army, all have the sacred duty before the Tsar and the *motherland to remain true to our duty and to our oath, and to maintain railway traffic and the flow of food.*

*Martin McCauley, **The Russian Revolution and the Soviet State** (Macmillan, 1975)*

The people in Petrograd now looked to the Duma politicians for leadership but as many of them did not wish to defy the Tsar they compromised; the Duma was dissolved but a Provisional Duma Committee remained in existence to restore order. It was clear that the politicians had been taken by surprise and were being 'led' by the will of the people. Members of the establishment, paralysed by fear, also pledged loyalty to this 'Provisional Government'. On the same day, the Workers' Group revived the Petrograd Soviet which pledged to restore order and food supplies.

Meanwhile the Tsar's train journey was blocked by 'unfriendly troops' and he was forced to make a detour to Pskov, where he arrived on 1 March. Nicholas's fate now lay with his generals. Their main aim was to win the war against Germany. Putting down internal disorder could weaken the front line and mutiny might spread. The generals favoured a ministry of Duma politicians as the easiest way to restore order in the rear. Nicholas agreed to this at the end of the day, but the following morning (2 March) Rodzianko, Chairman of the Duma Committee, made it clear that the people wanted the Tsar to abdicate. The senior generals, who had lost confidence in Nicholas's ability to rule, then all advised the Tsar to do so. They did this believing that the Duma leaders were in control and that revolution would be avoided by abdication. Abandoned by his generals, Nicholas had no real choice but to step down.

Two Duma politicians, Shilgun and Guchkov, also arrived in Pskov to demand the Tsar's abdication. They did, however, hope to save the monarchy and hoped the Tsar would step down in favour of his son, Alexis. But the Tsar would not because of his son's haemophilia; instead he designated Grand-Duke Michael as his heir. However, this discussion was academic; by the following day the Duma Committee had decided that the continuation of the monarchy in any form was unacceptable to the workers and soldiers of Petrograd and Grand-Duke

Michael was persuaded to stand aside. So ended 300 years of Romanov rule. Nicholas II broke down and wept.

Analysis

When the end came it was sudden, swift and, despite the many forecasts of doom, something of a surprise. Why did it happen when it did? What were the causes of this dramatic event? Obviously there are so many, the student can be forgiven for being unable to distinguish which are the more important ones. It might be instructive to begin by comparing 1917 with 1905. What were the similarities? What were the (crucial) differences?

The similarities are reasonably clear: in October 1905 and February 1917 discontent fuelled by defeat in war fused liberal political aspirations with the grievances of the proletariat (industrial working class). Workers and middle-class politicians came together to shake the monarchy. Nicholas was able to survive in 1905 because the war with Japan was over, he made timely concessions, and because he retained the support of the elite and the loyalty of the bulk of the army, which enabled him to use force to restore order and suppress discontent. The difference in 1917 was that all of these options were unavailable to him.

There are, then, important differences that distinguish 1917:
- the war was not over
- the army was not loyal
- the elite was prepared to sacrifice the Tsar.

As all three of these points are interrelated it is impossible to determine which of them is more important than the other.

Quite clearly the war was crucial – without it what happened could not have happened. Defeat in 1915 had alienated the liberal politicians; food and fuel shortages in 1916 had alienated all urban dwellers – the professional classes as well as the industrial workers. However, mass urban discontent could be contained by force and the liberals were always wary of unleashing a revolution. These groups could be controlled in 1905. What was crucially different in 1917 was the condition of the army.

During the course of the First World War nearly 15 million men were called up – about half were the victims of enemy action (2.4 million prisoners; 2.8 million wounded; 1.8 million killed). The loyal soldiers of 1914 (and more importantly, their loyal, upper-class officers) no longer existed in 1917. The soldiers in the army of 1917 were an unknown quantity whose loyalty and patriotism the generals and the Tsar could not be sure of. Moreover, the bulk of the trained army was in the front line facing the enemy. They did not mutiny: the Tsar was brought down by the 160,000 garrison troops of Petrograd. Of course, the garrison troops were not professional soldiers; they were not even trained soldiers; they were freshly drafted peasant recruits who were crammed into barracks designed to hold about 20,000. Rodzianko observed 'these of course were not soldiers but peasants taken directly from the plough'. Could they have been dealt with? The answer is hypothetical, but possibly yes. There must have been some loyal troops the government could rely on to restore order but removing them from the front to recapture Petrograd would have undoubtedly weakened the line against the Germans and jeopardised the war effort. Such action might have led to civil war and it might have failed. However, it should be observed that most of Russia was calm – the countryside was quiet, as indeed were most of the cities (though Moscow quickly fell to the revolutionaries after 27 February). It has been suggested that the situation was indeed manageable.

If this is the case, then the key factor becomes the decision of the elite to abandon Nicholas. The monarchy was so discredited by February 1917 that even committed monarchists had turned against it. No one was prepared to save the monarchy. The blame for this situation rests squarely with Nicholas II whose weakness and failure to make concessions earlier, say, in the autumn of 1916, deprived the monarchy of all support. The government was entirely discredited and under the guidance of 'that German woman', the Tsarina, had virtually disintegrated. Therefore it was the decision of the generals not to support Nicholas and not to restore order, that brought him down.

Had Nicholas embraced the Duma politicians, he would have probably retained the support of the elite, but this takes no account of the disaffection of the urban masses. Nevertheless, hypothesis played an important role in the revolution, in the form of fear of what might happen. The middle classes and the elite were driven by fear: fear of revolution, fear of the masses rising up and depriving them of their wealth and privileges. There was so much fear that the educated classes came to expect a revolution, even when it was not imminent. Accordingly, when mass unrest did break out, the Duma politicians and the generals were paralysed and did not know what to do. By removing the Tsar they thought they were preventing a revolution. They made the false assumption that after his removal things could only get better. In fact, the middle classes greeted the abdication with relief and, in many instances, delight. How wrong they were!

What the generals and politicians had done was to unleash the revolution they had sought to prevent. They came to be swept along by events, swept along by the aspirations of the masses. The people knew what they wanted; the elite did not know how to hold on to what it had. Once the Tsar was removed, the state was decapitated, authority collapsed, the whole structure of society began to unravel and a climate of disobedience developed. It was allowed to develop by paralysis at the top. The problem was that there was really no one at the top at all, there was a vacuum: no one was prepared to take the responsibility and use force to restore law and order.

The revolution was a spontaneous affair; unplanned and with no clear leadership. That does not mean to say that the revolution was not consciously willed; it was the result of many long-standing grievances and a determination by ordinary people to bring about real change and an improvement in their living and working conditions. It had little to do with the revolutionary parties. The motivation of the masses was very much their own; the revolution was a truly popular movement 'from below'. This was not going to be easily reconciled with the very different aspirations of the generals and the Duma politicians.

Essay

Why was the Tsar forced to abdicate in 1917?

Any discussion of the February Revolution requires you to consider the relative merits of long-term and short-term causes. Whichever you favour will take up the bulk of the essay.

If you take the view that the deeply-held long-term grievances of the peasants, workers and middle classes were ever present and that short-term factors were paramount in translating this mass discontent into a revolution, then the answer should really focus on the war – as this chapter does.

You will need a paragraph on the position in 1914 if only to show that, while discontent was widespread, the regime remained in control. Then you should go on to look at the failures in the war, both military and political, before tackling the actual events of February 1917. During the course of the essay your discussion might attempt to establish a hierarchy of causes or even a fundamental cause, if you feel you can identify one. Your conclusion would then probably point forward, to indicate that the removal of the Tsar did not in fact solve the problems facing the people of Russia, though it certainly brought them all to the surface.

CHAPTER FIVE

WHY DID THE PROVISIONAL GOVERNMENT FAIL?

Objectives

⊿ To determine why the Provisional Government failed
⊿ To show how it was that the Bolsheviks took their place.

It is probably wrong to talk of a single Russian Revolution – or even of the two, February and October – because there were many revolutions. 'Every social group, every nationality, every region, every town', every village, had its own revolution' (Christopher Read), but as yet historians have not given sufficient attention to what was happening at grassroots level and we do not have a complete picture. For our purposes we will focus on Petrograd, on the **Provisional Government** and that city's **Soviet**. However, we will not lose sight of the fact that what happened at the top was constantly affected by spontaneous changes from below. In many ways the politicians were swept along by the aspirations of the ordinary people throughout 1917. Indeed the main reason why the Provisional Government failed was because it tried to resist the demands of the people.

Quite obviously there was so much going on in Russia in 1917 that it is very difficult to produce a coherent summary of events. In this brief overview it should be appreciated that the headings are for convenience and in many instances events overlapped or were simultaneous.

KEY TERMS

The Provisional Government was the government that replaced Nicholas. It evolved from the Duma and consisted mainly of Duma politicians. It was therefore not representative but it was accepted as it was only 'provisional' until the election of the Constituent Assembly which would determine the new constitution. Initially fronted by Prince George Lvov, from July it was headed by Alexander Kerensky. Its legitimacy, however, was dubious and its hold on power tenuous.

The Petrograd Soviet was the Soviet (or council) of workers' and soldiers' deputies. It consisted of 3,000 elected representatives, but business was handled by an executive committee, and later a bureau of 24 representing the main socialist parties on a quota basis. The Soviet had real power: it controlled Petrograd and in particular the garrison. However, the socialist politicians (mainly Mensheviks and SRs) were prepared to allow Russia to go through a bourgeois phase (see key term Marxism, page 53), content to merely 'supervise' the Provisional Government.

Summary of events

Dual power?

It used to be thought that the Provisional Government had responsibility but no power, and that the Petrograd Soviet possessed the power but would not exercise any responsibility. The picture today is not quite so simple, as historians now believe that the Provisional Government did have a 'window of opportunity' (March, April) to satisfy the masses, and in any case fear of counter-revolution from the Right bound the two bodies together. However, there was never any real possibility of the Duma politicians – the men of property and business – satisfying the aspirations of the ordinary people. These men were not revolutionaries; they were there to prevent revolution.

Radical socialists urged the Soviet to take control straightaway and workers and soldiers immediately rallied to its support. On 1 March the Petrograd Soviet issued Order No. 1 which curtailed officers' authority in the army. However, the majority of the Soviet – Mensheviks and Socialist Revolutionaries – favoured a government of Duma politicians. They contented themselves with control of the vital services, railways, the post (and increasingly the army) through workers' and soldiers' committees. Indeed many socialists believed that Russia was not yet ready for socialism as it had still to go through a bourgeois phase. Thus the Provisional Government came into being headed by Prince George Lvov, with Pavel Miliukov as foreign minister, Alexander Guchkov as war minister and the only socialist, Alexander Kerensky, as justice minister. Initially the government was inundated with expressions of support, but it was soon to forfeit this support by failing to solve the country's problems.

Institutional change

Inspired by classical liberal philosophy, the government issued a host of well-meaning reforms: freedom of the press, speech and of association; no discrimination on grounds of nationality or religion; the release of political prisoners and the abolition of the death penalty. Whether or not it was sensible for the government to deprive itself of coercive power in a climate of growing disobedience is very questionable. Moreover, it found it much easier to sweep away the old order than put anything in its place.

Other institutional changes were largely forced upon the government by circumstances. The disappearance of the Tsarist police force left the Duma politicians with little option other than to try to bolster the rather feeble local militia. Similarly those scions of the old regime, the provincial governors, had to go. Lvov put the chairmen of the local *zemstvo* boards in their place as 'commissars' but this device was unpopular with the peasantry. The Provisional Government intended the full democratisation of local government but by the time the politicians had worked out the legal niceties of the scheme (August!), it had lost control of the localities completely. 'Committees of Public Organisations' had sprung up in most localities – peasant committees were established to organise food supplies and to consider land reform, workers established factory committees, nationalities their own committees, and soldiers established army committees – all designed to improve conditions. In addition, 'a complex network of regional, city and suburban Soviets were elected to represent workers and in some areas soldiers and peasants' (Edward Acton). A Central Executive Committee of all Soviets met as early as April. From the beginning it would appear that the Provisional Government did not control the country – the people did. Faced with this wealth of local initiative the government was under pressure to deliver change from the very beginning and two key issues come to the fore from the start – peace and land.

War and peace

A serious rift developed between the government and the Soviet over the issue of the war. Basically it is wrong to talk of a peace party on the left because no one wanted to surrender to the Germans. The issue was whether or not the war should be prosecuted vigorously with offensives and annexations (the position of the Provisional Government) or whether or not it should be fought for self-defence – 'revolutionary defencism', as it was called (the position of the Soviet). The Soviet seemed to be undermining the war effort: Order No. 2 on 6 March recognised the right of soldiers to replace commanders and on 14 March the Soviet issued an appeal to the world for a democratic peace.

Miliukov and the government, however, were strongly committed to the war – for three reasons:

1 Nationalist sentiment – there was a strong patriotic desire among the middle and upper classes to gain victory and to win territory, especially Constantinople (Istanbul).

2 The government was committed to its treaties with its allies. Liberal politicians wanted to retain the friendship of the liberal democracies of Britain and France and it needed their aid.

3 Defeat would give Germany control of Europe and lead to the collapse of the Empire.

In addition, it could be argued that the war was a way of maintaining government authority, deflecting domestic demands for reform and delaying the calling of the Constituent Assembly. It certainly looks as though these factors were important in Kadet thinking.

The Soviet position was rather muddled. Calling for peace, undermining discipline in the army and at the same time agreeing to the continuation of the war, all seem rather contradictory.

A major crisis blew up between 18 and 22 April when a secret note by Miliukov was made public. In it he reassured Allies that the Provisional Government did not support the Soviet call for a renunciation of imperialist war aims by all combatants. This led to street demonstrations and a government reshuffle. Miliukov and Guchkov resigned and on 5 May the First Coalition government was formed with six Soviet socialists (three SRs, two Mensheviks and a Popular Socialist). Remarkably, these moderate socialists actually agreed to an offensive in June (the so-called Kerensky Offensive of 18 June) but this collapsed in the first week in July and had important political consequences in the capital (see below). It was quite clear that the army no longer had any stomach for offensive action. Even so, the Kadet politicians of the Provisional Government remained committed to the aggressive prosecution of the war.

Peasants and the land

War and the land question were inextricably linked. If land were given to the peasants, soldiers (peasants in uniform) would desert and return to their village to secure their share. In principle the majority of ministers accepted that there had to be far-reaching land reform but it had to be done in a legal and systematic way. This, in turn, could only be done by the legitimately elected representatives of the people in the Constituent Assembly. Faced with an increasing number of illegal land seizures, Victor Chernov, the SR Minister of Agriculture (from May), tried to transfer some land to peasant committees; but it was too little too late. In any event the government could not agree on how to handle such a complex issue. For instance, there was the important question of compensation to both landowners and banks. Meanwhile the peasant committees took matters into their own hands and there was nothing the government could do about it. Apart from a brief decline during the harvest period, peasant unrest became ever more widespread from September and in the face of the rising level of violence and land seizures the Kadets began to side with the land-owners. By the autumn the government had lost control of the countryside (if it ever did have any real control).

As far as food supply was concerned, the government did establish a grain monopoly on 25 March and a system of food committees to fix prices. However, the peasants had no incentive to sell at fixed prices. A rationing system was announced on 29 April but two months later it had still not been implemented. At the end of August the government doubled grain prices to encourage the peasantry but this only succeeded in fuelling inflation. In truth, the liberals in the cabinet were reluctant to undertake the degree of state regulation that was necessary in this crisis. This had a dramatic impact on the cities.

Workers and the factories

The end of Imperial Russia heralded an unprecedented wave of labour unrest with demands for higher wages and better working conditions – in particular the eight-hour day which was conceded by employers in Petrograd on 10 March, decreed by the Soviet in Moscow 11 days later and became a reality throughout the country by the end of April. However, these developments did not lead to an improvement in the economy. It continued to deteriorate and the problems that had helped to bring down the Tsar worsened dramatically. The railway system began to grind to a halt, leading to an even greater shortage of fuel and raw materials and a dramatic decline in industrial production. Food shortages and rampant inflation created immense hardship.

As far as factory closures are concerned, recent research suggests that workers and employers were conciliatory until the middle of the year. Thereafter profits fell sharply and employers concluded that concessions had not worked. At the same time, workers became more militant as their circumstances became more desperate. Thus lock-outs and worker takeovers were a response to industrial breakdown rather than its cause.

The Bolsheviks' false dawn

The revolutionary politicians had been taken completely by surprise by the collapse of Tsardom. The Bolsheviks, in particular, had been slow off the mark and the Soviets had come to be dominated by their rivals, the Mensheviks and the Social Revolutionaries. Lenin, the leader of the Bolsheviks, was in fact stuck in Switzerland but the Germans were happy to send him back to Russia to undermine the war effort. He was transported in a sealed train via Scandinavia and arrived in Petrograd on 3 April. The next day he issued his 'April Theses', in which he stated:

◢ Source

In our attitude towards the war not the slightest concession must be made to 'revolutionary defencism', for even under the new government of Lvov and Co. the war on Russia's part unquestionably remains a predatory imperialist war owing to the capitalist nature of that government . . .

In view of the undoubted honesty of the mass of the rank-and-file believers in revolutionary defencism, who accept the war as a necessity only and not as a means of conquest; in view of the fact that they are being deceived by the bourgeoisie, it is necessary thoroughly, persistently and patiently to explain the indissoluble connection between capital and the imperialist war, and to prove that it is impossible to end the war by a truly democratic, non-coercive peace without the overthrow of capital.

The widespread propaganda of this view among the army on active service must be organised . . .

No support must be given to the Provisional Government; the utter falsity of all its promises must be exposed, particularly of those relating to the renunciation of annexations. Exposure, and not the unpardonable illusion-breeding 'demand' that this government, a government of capitalists, should cease to be an imperialist government.

It must be explained to the masses that the Soviet of Workers' Deputies is the only possible form of revolutionary government and that therefore our task is, as long as this government submits to the influence of the bourgeoisie, to present a patient, systematic, and persistent explanation of its errors and tactics, an explanation especially adapted to the practical needs of the masses.

*'The April Theses', from Lenin **Selected Works***

Thus Lenin declared war on the Provisional Government and all who supported it. In addition, he called for the confiscation of all private estates, the nationalisation of the land and Soviet control of banks, production and distribution. However, it took him a while to convince his own party of this policy. Despite catchy slogans – such as 'Peace, Land and Bread' and 'All Power to the Soviets' – the Bolsheviks made only slow headway and were in a minority in most popular committees until the late summer. Mensheviks and SRs controlled the soldiers' committees; the SRs controlled those of the peasants; the Mensheviks, the Trade Unions. In June these two parties dominated the First All-Russian Congress of Soviets. In fact, the Bolsheviks only had about one-eighth of the delegates yet they were beginning to make some headway in the factory committees and among the armed forces.

By July the Provisional Government was deeply unpopular and the Soviet's association with it was beginning to damage socialist politicians as well. A demonstration called by the Soviet Congress on 18 June to back Soviet policy turned into an anti-government rally, but the real crunch came two weeks later on the **July Days** (2–4 July). These demonstrations had a lot to do with disaffection among the armed forces (with Kerensky's Offensive). Troops, and sailors from Kronstadt, organised an armed demonstration aimed at overthrowing the Provisional Government. Although the Bolsheviks did not organise this rising, it is significant that the demonstrators looked to them for leadership which, however, was not forthcoming. The attempted uprising deteriorated into a shambles and the government was able to blame the Bolsheviks, denounce Lenin as a German agent (he fled to Finland), destroy their press and arrest their leaders (including Trotsky who had just joined the party). The Bolsheviks looked finished, but then they were saved by the 'Kornilov Affair'.

The Kornilov Affair

In the aftermath of the mass insubordination which had ruined the June offensive, Kerensky restored the death penalty. The Kadet leadership was frustrated by the government's lack of coercive power and became convinced that the army must be used to halt the revolution. By 18 July Miliukov was calling for a military dictatorship. The Kornilov Affair has to be seen in this context. However, the truth is that the government did not have any coercive power. The February Revolution had smashed traditional authority beyond repair and the High Command and officers could only rely on the voluntary consent of their men – and the men wanted peace, land and bread.

Kerensky formed a Second Coalition government on 24 July, which although containing a socialist majority was still dominated by the four Kadet members. In August he called a State Conference of both left- and right-wing representatives in Moscow (12–15 August) to generate national unity in the face of the crisis following the offensive and to shore up his own position. The Conference made no decisions but Kerensky emerged as the dominant political personality. General Kornilov, the new Commander-in-Chief, who had replaced Brusilov, emerged as the darling of the middle classes.

The precise details of the 'Kornilov revolt' are unclear but what is clear is that Kornilov was going to use reliable troops to suppress a rumoured Bolshevik uprising, restore order in the capital and discipline in the army. It appears that Kerensky had approved this action but seems to have come to believe that Kornilov intended replacing him. Accordingly he switched sides, mobilised the Petrograd Soviet, armed the Red Guards and released (and armed) the Bolsheviks. Kornilov was thrown into confusion by this 'betrayal'; but determined to press on; however his troops abandoned him and he was arrested (1 September).

If the details of the affair are not wholly clear, the consequences are. Kerensky was completely discredited – he had lost the support of the Right without gaining any support on the Left, and discipline in the army now deteriorated at an alarming rate. A power vacuum had opened up at the top, and the scene was set for the Bolshevik takeover.

The October Revolution

In September the Bolsheviks began to make some real political headway. On 9 September they won the support of the majority in the Petrograd Soviet and on 25 September Trotsky was elected its chairman. From Finland Lenin urged the seizure of power.

◢ Source

The Bolsheviks, having obtained a majority in the Soviets of Workers' and Soldiers' Deputies of both capitals, can and must take state power into their own hands.

They can do so because the active majority of revolutionary elements in the two chief cities is large enough to carry the people with it, to overcome our opponents' resistance to smash them, and to gain and retain power. For the Bolsheviks, by immediately proposing a democratic peace, by immediately giving the land to the peasants and by re-establishing the democratic institutions and liberties which have been distorted and shattered by Kerensky, will form a government which nobody will be able to overthrow.

The majority of the people are on our side ... By seizing power both in Moscow and in Petrograd at once (it doesn't matter which comes first, possibly Moscow), we shall win absolutely and unquestionably.

Lenin in a letter, 12–14 September 1917

However, the Bolshevik Central Committee rejected Lenin's plea at this stage so he returned to Petrograd in early October to persuade the party in person. On 10 October he addressed the Central Committee and they agreed to consider an armed uprising, but it took another meeting six days later to get an unequivocal endorsement. Even so, two influential Bolsheviks – Lev Kamenev and Gregori Zinoviev – opposed Lenin's position and actually published their objections on 18 October. Lenin was resolute and he found a true ally in Trotsky.

The key to Bolshevik success proved to be the Military Revolutionary Committee (MRC) which came into being between 9 and 16 October. It was created by the Petrograd Soviet to defend the city if the Germans attacked (by this time they were beyond Riga). 'The relatively legitimate task of preparing the city's defences provided an excellent smokescreen to conceal preparations for the seizure of power' (Read). Kerensky does not appear to have taken the Bolsheviks' threat seriously until on 24 October when he finally moved against them, thus precipitating their insurrection. The whole affair was remarkably bloodless as the majority of soldiers simply did nothing but look on. On 21 and 22 October the MRC was able to assert its authority over the Petrograd garrison and two days later Government troops were persuaded to give up control of key points – bridges and the like – and Kerensky's power just melted away. Lenin urged more decisive action and on the night of 24–25 October Trotsky organised the occupation of the central telephone exchange, railway stations, the central post office and other key installations. The Winter Palace, where the Provisional Government was in session, was captured after resistance stopped in the early hours of 26 October.

Meanwhile Kerensky had slipped away. It was all over in 36 hours, with the minimum of bloodshed and violence. The Bolsheviks had occupied a political vacuum. Lenin addressed the Second All-Russian Congress and while many were appalled at what had happened, the majority of delegates supported him. However, occupying the seat of government was one thing, being able to govern was another. The Bolsheviks had to consolidate their power. The Revolution had only just begun.

Analysis

So why did the Provisional Government fail? There are three elements which we might identify in explanation:

- the failings of the Provisional government itself (*i.e.* its own mistakes)
- the people's revolution (*i.e.* the aspirations and actions of the ordinary people which completely undermined the government's authority)
- the opposition of the Bolsheviks (*i.e.* Lenin's determination to overthrow the Provisional Government).

Let us look at each of these in turn:

The failings of the Provisional Government

A number of criticisms have been made of the Provisional Government. The liberal politicians:

⊿ had little understanding of the workings of government;
⊿ wasted time over legal niceties;
⊿ were too aware of their provisional nature;
⊿ were themselves bitterly divided;
⊿ were reluctant to use force to impose their will;
⊿ were unable to control the Soviets;
⊿ could not manage the economy;
⊿ failed to distribute the land;
⊿ wished to continue the war;
⊿ upheld the interest of the bourgeoisie;
⊿ betrayed the masses;
⊿ failed to call the Constituent Assembly.

There is a great deal of truth in all these charges but they miss the point. The point is that too much was expected of the Provisional Government in too short a time. Soldiers wanted an end to the war; peasants wanted the land; workers wanted better conditions; the politically articulate wanted freedom of association, press and so on; different nationalities wanted self-determination; the Allies wanted an offensive against the Germans. Any government would have found all these aspirations difficult to fulfil in peacetime let alone during a difficult war. Moreover, the government was only provisional (clearly the failure to call the Constituent Assembly was a major mistake) and its power was undermined by the Soviets. Thus it can be argued that it faced an impossible task.

From February onwards the central government was simply drained of power as ordinary people took matters into their own hands. The Tsarist system had held Russia together; with the Tsar gone the power structure collapsed. Traditional authority had been smashed beyond repair and a climate of disobedience took its place. The government had to comply with the wishes of the masses (and quickly) otherwise it was doomed. There was a honeymoon period, perhaps until May, when the government could have acted, but by June it was over. For this reason the June offensive was meant to restore the government's prestige. Its failure had significant political implications. In particular, it was a personal calamity for Kerensky whose self-confidence and judgement suffered as a result. The people increasingly ignored the Provisional Government and when Kerensky fell out with Kornilov in

August (another major mistake – he feared the Right and ignored the Left) he succeeded in alienating the army. What little power the government had left, evaporated. The government not only failed to accede to the people's demands, it consciously tried to resist them. This was the policy of the Kadets.

There is much truth in Lenin's oft-quoted parody of Provisional Government policy: 'Wait until the Constituent Assembly for land. Wait until the end of the war for the Constituent Assembly. Wait until total victory for the end of the war.' The Kadets did not want to distribute land until the Constituent Assembly was called and as peasant demands became more radical they sided with the landowners. The Kadets were opposed to the state regulation of the economy on philosophical grounds. The Kadets fully supported the war even after the failure of the summer offensive. They wished to halt the revolution and favoured a military coup to restore discipline and to smash the soviets. And the Kadets deliberately postponed the calling of the Constituent Assembly because they knew they would be swamped by the socialist parties. (This proved to be correct: in November they only polled 4.7 per cent.) Looked at in this light, it is not surprising the Provisional Government failed. Given that the Kadets consciously wished to resist the aspirations of the ordinary people but lacked any power to resist them, it is remarkable that the Provisional Government lasted as long as it did.

The people's revolution

Resistance to popular demands was impossible in the climate of 1917. In the absence of coercion, the peasants, workers and soldiers could simply disobey landlords, managers and officers, thereby destroying the authority of the politicians in government. No one would do as they were told! But this was not simply blind obstinacy; the people had their own aspirations. And they did not need politicians – even socialist ones – to tell them what they wanted.

The **peasantry** believed the land should belong to those who worked it. The seizure of private land was usually planned and coordinated through the village commune. The peasants also sought equitable justice, local government officials elected by themselves and free education. 'The goals, methods and rhythm of peasant actions during 1917 were their own' (Acton).

The peasant revolution began slowly and did not really get under way until the autumn. Initially the peasants organised themselves into committees, sought to bring unsown land back into productive use, withdrew their labour from landlords and intervened in the management of estates where landowners looked as though they were asset stripping. The government tried to steer a middle course between the landowners and peasants (which was impossible) and after July tried to take a firmer line against the latter. For instance, on 8 July the government confirmed that land seizures were completely impermissible pending the decision of the Constituent Assembly. The subsequent decline in peasant 'incidents' in August was deceptive as the majority were working on the harvest. Although the position of Soviet historians has always been that all the peasants rose in revolt in September and October, it seems likely that this is an exaggeration. There were serious disturbances but these were largely confined to about a dozen provinces and carried out by a minority of the peasantry. Many peasants showed remarkable patience and were prepared to wait for a legal transfer of land but only because they felt that there was a new environment in which their wishes would be fulfilled. However, the patience of others was running out and at the time of the October Revolution, direct action was coming to the fore, and there was little the government could do about it. In short, the Provisional Government could not control events in the countryside.

Most historical research has focused on the **proletariat**, though in truth the workers were not as important as the soldiery in terms of the collapse of government authority. In particular, the phenomenon of the Soviets has generated much attention. There were 300 of these within three months, 600 by August and 900 by October, but in reality they were controlled by an elite of activists and for many workers, the unions and factory committees were the organs through which their demands were made and met. What did the workers want? They wanted better conditions: improved wages, a shorter working day, an end to the authoritarian factory structure and an end to the humiliating treatment meted out by management. In the aftermath of the February Revolution many of these demands were met and unpopular managers were 'purged'.

Initially, factory committees were quite moderate in their requests.

However, the improvement in working conditions did not bring an improvement in the economy; it continued to deteriorate and as it did so worker demands became more extreme as workers moved from their own agenda to a reactive one. Rising prices, shortages of raw materials and problems of food supply led to an increasing number of strikes from May onwards (peaking in September). However, strikes did not keep the factories open and after the 'July Days' the workers in Petrograd faced mass redundancies and the possibility of counter-revolution. 1917 then was not a glorious episode for the proletariat; it was a growing nightmare. In this light the increasing radicalisation of worker demands takes on a different hue and the takeover of factories – workers' control – should be interpreted as a last ditch act of desperation to save jobs, rather than a manifestation of some radical agenda. Motives remained economic though politicisation went on apace. However, workers were true to issues rather than parties and they were prepared to support anyone who could restore the economy. Thus they had little time for the Provisional Government and if their leadership in the Soviet failed, they were prepared to support new leaders here too. It is in this context that Bolshevik success should be seen.

Where did all this leave the Provisional Government? Quite clearly it was powerless to resist initial worker demands and powerless to prevent their increasing radicalisation. The responsibility for the collapsing economy must also rest with the government, though all the problems that we have mentioned were inherited. However, they got worse, rather than better. Worker demands did not help the economy – working less hours and being paid more money cannot have helped company viability – but much of subsequent worker intransigence was, as we have seen, the result of economic collapse rather than its cause. The Provisional Government's failure to manage the economy lost it the support of the working class. As in the countryside, the Provisional Government had little control in the cities, and the main reason for this is because it did not control the soldiers either. Thus by far the most significant group, as far as government authority was concerned, were the soldiers. It was with them that the fate of the government rested.

The **soldiers**, who were largely peasants in uniform, naturally shared the wish for land reform but they also wanted to transform traditional military discipline. They wanted representative committees, the dismissal of unpopular officers and more humane treatment. These changes occurred almost instantaneously throughout the Empire and were reflected in the Petrograd Soviet's Orders No. 1 and No. 2 (which, though for the Petrograd garrison only, had widespread repercussions across Russia). Generally speaking, the changes were 'spontaneous, orderly and responsible', and symptomatic of a 'massive, self-generating revolutionary movement from below' (Read).

Initially, the government adopted a conciliatory attitude and proclaimed a limited Declaration of Soldiers' Rights (11 May). The soldiers also wanted an early end to the war and did not want to conduct offensive operations. There was, however, an inherent contradiction in this position. The Germans were not simply going to go away! This attitude accounted for the failure of the June Offensive, and the rebellious garrison troops in early July. In the aftermath the government tried to tighten up discipline by reintroducing the death penalty (12 July) and reports from the front in mid-August indicated that the situation was quite stable. In fact, the incidence of desertion (before October) has been much exaggerated and the soldiers were committed to stopping the German advance.

However, the Kornilov Affair destroyed any trust that there might have been. The incident was interpreted as an attack on soldiers' rights. Now no one supported the government and relations between soldiers and officers sunk to an all-time low. The soldiers were tired and hungry and had little faith in either the High Command or the possibility of victory. As with the peasantry, this disaffection was generated by the soldiers themselves not by outside political agitators. Hunger was more powerful than propaganda. By October the whole army was being swept by a 'virtual tidal wave . . . of self-assertion by the soldier mass on behalf of peace regardless of consequences or conditions' (Wildman). Increasingly radical resolutions were passed by the soldiers and a refusal to obey orders became widespread. The Russian army was disintegrating and once again there was absolutely nothing the government could do about it. Moreover, without military force the government was impotent.

Of course the leading arbiter of national politics was the Petrograd garrison, and garrison troops tended to be more radical than those in the front line. The soldiers would have supported any government which was prepared to carry out the policies they favoured (peace, land, democracy and so on) but the growing inability, or unwillingness, of the Provisional Government to carry out these policies meant that when the government was threatened the garrison did nothing to save it.

It would appear, then, that the increasingly radical challenge to traditional authority by the peasants, workers and soldiers dictated the course of the revolution and sealed the fate of the Provisional Government. Once it became clear that the government was not going to fulfil their wishes, the ordinary people took direct action through their committees. But there was a limit to what these committees could do: they could not end the war, restore the economy or ensure food supplies throughout Russia. The people needed a government of politicians who were prepared to carry out the people's policies. They needed a party with a programme that coincided with theirs – this is where the Bolsheviks come in.

The Bolshevik takeover

If we look at the state of the political parties in February 1917 we would have to say that the Bolsheviks were the least likely party to take control. The Kadets dominated the government but were unable to attract mass support as there was an inherent contradiction in wanting universal suffrage and serving the interests of the propertied few. They suffered a precipitate decline. The Soviets were dominated by the Mensheviks and the Social Revolutionaries – the former had considerable support among the proletariat, the latter among peasantry and both had support among the soldiers. The Bolsheviks were behind all these parties with a membership of 10,000; and things did not get much better for them. Lenin's return in April generated more interest and his position – 'no support to the Provisional Government', and no collaboration with other socialist parties – was unique and proved to be valuable later. However, up to the July Days the Bolshevik Party had made little progress and their suppression after this episode seemed to herald their demise. Yet remarkably, from this time on their political strength began to grow as they came to be seen as the one party untainted by collaboration with the Provisional Government.

This growth in support in August predated the Kornilov Affair but that event proved to be the real turning-point. What had been a trickle became a flood in September as more and more people turned to the Bolsheviks as their next best hope. By October membership had ballooned to 300,000.

However there is an important point to be made here. People (and we are mainly talking about workers and some soldiers here – the Bolsheviks were always weak among the peasantry) were turning to the Bolsheviks not because they were becoming committed to Bolshevism, but because they had become dissatisfied with the socialist parties which had worked with the Provisional Government and failed to deliver on the fundamental issues of peace, land and bread. The Mensheviks and the Social Revolutionaries were discredited by their collaboration; the Mensheviks in particular suffered a dramatic collapse. This was because they had set themselves against popular opinion by refusing to create a soviet government. This was a significant missed opportunity. So the Bolsheviks inherited the people's hopes somewhat by default; they did not hold out 'a new vision of the revolution', but rather 'a more speedy realisation of the original one' (Wildman).

The fact that the Bolsheviks were able to absorb such a dramatic increase in membership and support belies the old view that they were a ruthless, rigid, centralised, disciplined, streamlined machine. At this stage they were in fact a flexible, fluid organisation and while Lenin's prestige was immense, he did not have the control Soviet historians used to have us believe. In addition, the party's propaganda and policies did not educate and persuade the masses, rather they evoked a response because they coincided with the masses' view. They did not create the people's programme, they merely articulated it.

What Lenin brought to the movement was a programme distinct from the other parties and an unstoppable drive to seize power. Whether or not he was behind the July Days is a moot point but in the autumn he saw a real opportunity and although his timing was wrong in September, without him it is unlikely that the Bolsheviks would have taken power in October. It is still likely that the Provisional Government under Kerensky would have collapsed – it had no support and no power at all – but what would have replaced it is anybody's guess, though a soviet government (*i.e.* a coalition of socialists) was the only real alternative. Kerensky's blunders over Kornilov and finally on 24 October when he tried to suppress the Bolsheviks, ensured their victory. In many ways he initiated the insurrection by forcing the Bolsheviks to defend themselves. But while the October Revolution bore all the classic hallmarks of a *coup d'état*, it was more than that – it was a response to the popular movement. The troops stood by and allowed the Bolsheviks to take over – in the name of the soviets, in the name of the people. But this turned out to be a massive deception.

Thus it can be argued that the Provisional Government was almost doomed to failure from the start. The propertied classes had removed the Tsar to prevent a revolution but their vision of a liberal democracy which would maintain their position of privilege in no way corresponded to the wishes of the people. Perhaps it was intellectual arrogance that made the bourgeoisie feel the people could not have an agenda? In any event, the people did have an agenda (peace, land, bread, etc.) and this was the revolution 'from below'. The government failed to respond to the people's wishes and even came to resist them. But it had no power to do so. Power rested with the people but they in turn needed a responsive government.

Eventually, after the failure of the Mensheviks and SRs in coalition, many turned to the Bolsheviks. After August Kerensky's government had no power and Lenin stepped into his place in October. Whereas the people saw the Bolsheviks as a vehicle for achieving their aims, for Lenin popular support was a vehicle for achieving his messianic vision of world revolution and world socialism. Accordingly, there was bound to be a dramatic clash between these two perceptions. 'Where the people thought they were taking power for themselves, they were actually handing it over to a new, authoritarian leadership with almost un-limited aims' (Read). This became clear as the Bolsheviks struggled to retain power.

Essay

Why did the Provisional Government fail?

There is no single right answer to this but clearly the failings of the Provisional Government, the people's agenda and the actions of the Bolsheviks are all key elements worthy of paragraphs. Do not be afraid to adopt your own position on this provided you have enough evidence to back up your argument.

Documentary exercises

1

Document A

The April Theses

Conference appeals to democracy to support the Provisional Government without assuming responsibility for all the work of the government, as long as the government steadfastly confirms and expands the gains of the revolution and so long as its foreign policy is based on the renunciation of ambitions of territorial expansion.

At the same time, Conference appeals to the revolutionary democracy of Russia to be prepared, while organising and rallying its forces around the Soviets of Workers' and Soldiers' Deputies, to vitiate all efforts by the government to escape the control exercised by democracy, or to evade the fulfilment of the obligations it has assumed.

Resolution of support for the Provisional Government by the All-Russian Conference of Soviets, 5 April 1917

Document B
Lenin's April Theses (see page 93)

Document C
In yesterday's issue of Pravda Comrade Lenin published his 'theses'. They represent the personal opinion of Comrade Lenin and by publishing them Comrade Lenin did something which is the duty of every outstanding public man – to submit to the judgement of the revolutionary democracy of Russia his understanding of current events.

. . . As regards Comrade Lenin's general line, it appears to us unacceptable inasmuch as it proceeds from the assumption that the bourgeois-democratic revolution has been

completed *and it builds on the immediate transformation of this revolution into a Socialist revolution. The tactics that follow from such analysis are greatly at variance with the tactics defended by the representatives of* Pravda *at the All-Russian Congress both against the official leaders of the Soviet and against the Mensheviks who dragged the Soviet to the Right.*

Lev Kamenev, 'Our Differences' **Pravda***, 8 April 1917*

a Explain the terms 'Soviets of Workers' and Soldiers' Deputies' (document A), and 'revolutionary defencism' (document B). *6 marks*

b In document B in what ways, and why, does Lenin seek to change the stance of the All-Russian Conference of Soviets as expressed in document A? *8 marks*

c For what reasons is Kamenev in document C opposed to Lenin's revolutionary strategy as outlined in the 'April Theses'? *8 marks*

d How important are the 'April Theses' in explaining the successful seizure of power by the Bolsheviks in the autumn of 1917? *8 marks*

Oxford and Cambridge Examination Board (1991)

2 The seizure of power

Document D
Lenin's letter of September 1917 (see page 96)

Document E

We are most profoundly convinced that to declare at once an armed uprising would mean to stake not only the fate of our party, but also the fate of the Russian and the international revolution ... The strength of our adversary is greater than it appears ... The strength of the proletarian party, of course, is very considerable, but the decisive question is, is the mood among the workers and soldiers of the capital really such, that they themselves see salvation already only in street fighting and are bursting to go on to the streets? No. This mood does not exist ...

The party of the proletariat will grow, its programme will become clearer to even wider masses ... And there is only one way that it can nullify its successes in present circumstances, and that is by taking the initiative for an uprising itself and in so doing subjecting the proletariat to the blows of the whole united counter-revolution, supported by petit-bourgeois democracy.

We raise a warning voice against this ruinous policy.

Kamenev and Zinoviev, 11 October 1917

a Explain the references to 'the Soviets of Workers' and Soldiers' Deputies' (document D) and to 'the international revolution' (document E).   *6 marks*

b Consult documents D and E. Why were Lenin's proposals opposed by his colleagues Kamenev and Zinoviev?   *8 marks*

c Do documents D and E provide convincing evidence of the extent of popular support enjoyed by the Bolsheviks by October 1917?   *8 marks*

d How far does the evidence provided by passages D and E explain the Bolsheviks' rise to power by October 1917?   *8 marks*

Oxford and Cambridge Examination Board (1990)

CHAPTER SIX

HOW DID THE BOLSHEVIKS CONSOLIDATE THEIR POWER 1917–24?

Objectives

◢ To consider the course of events – the Civil War, dictatorship and the New Economic Policy

◢ To analyse how the Bolsheviks were able to hold on to and consolidate their power

By the early 1920s Russia was in the authoritarian grip of a one-party dictatorship. The Communist Party, as the Bolsheviks had become, was a centralised, coercive body with a narrow band of support mainly from bureaucrats. It had a ruthless leadership which was ideologically motivated to hold on to power no matter what the cost in terms of popularity. This was a dramatic contrast to the position in 1917 when the party came to power enjoying a broad base of support among workers and soldiers who saw in it the best hope for fulfilling the aims of the popular revolution. Quite how the Bolshevik Party hijacked it and went off in an authoritarian direction is just one aspect of this chapter. Our main consideration though is how it could have done so and survived. After all, all sense of authority had been destroyed and yet the Bolsheviks survived the collapse of the economy, the alienation of the peasants, civil war, foreign intervention, nationalist secession, uprisings, splits, famine – and emerged with an iron grip on the political life of the country, having destroyed the popular revolution. This was a remarkable and surprising development.

Summary of events

Early days

The early days of the Bolshevik Revolution were the most democratic as the party had little real control over the country or events. The leadership had expected world revolution and had made little provision for ruling Russia after seizing power; so it had few specific plans. Nevertheless on 26 October decrees were passed on land and peace but slogans rather than substance characterised Bolshevik government in the early days.

Although there was serious fighting in Moscow (with a thousand casualties) the Bolsheviks and their catchphrase of 'all power to the Soviets' found an immediate echo in many major cities and towns. By means of revolutionary committees, which controlled the Soviets, Bolshevik power spread. By the end of November most of northern and central European Russia was under the control of the Soviet government. It was, however, a different story in the countryside, remote areas and non-Russian homelands. As early as December General Kornilov was gathering a 'volunteer army' of White Forces in the Don Cossack region to defy the government.

The elections to the Constituent Assembly took place in November – and the results were not quite what the Bolsheviks hoped for:

Social Revolutionaries (SRs)	48.1% *
Bolsheviks	24%
Kadets	4.7%
Mensheviks	4.1% †
Unaccounted	10.2%
Others	8.9%

* Including Ukrainian SRs
† Including Georgian Mensheviks

Quite clearly the SRs were the winners, the beneficiaries of enormous rural support. However, the Bolsheviks had considerable support where it mattered – in the military areas on the Northern and Western Fronts, in the Petrograd and Moscow military districts, in the Baltic fleet, among the civilians of Moscow and Petrograd; and although they only commanded a majority in six other provinces, it was enough to survive. Over 10 million people had voted for them and this was a large enough constituency from which to draw support. In any event, at this point few were aware of what the Bolsheviks really stood for.

The results did prompt Lenin to negotiate a coalition and he astutely split the SRs, bringing some left-wingers into the government (9 December). Thus he could claim that the government represented the vast majority of the people and he was easily able to dissolve the

Constituent Assembly by force when it met (5–6 January 1918). The effectiveness of the use of force and the acquiescence of their opponents (who above all feared counter-revolution) was a lesson not lost on the Bolsheviks.

As we have already indicated, Lenin had given little thought to economic strategy before October. As far as the peasants were concerned, Lenin's decree on land (which was in effect SR legislation and won many of them over to the government) simply legalised peasant seizures, many of which were already taking place. The government was thereby forced to accept the destruction of large manorial estates and the extension of the inefficient strip system which it did not really favour. Similarly, in industrial affairs the government had to allow workers to have control over the factories. This was not necessarily Bolshevik policy either but in the first six months or so the government had little coercive power and had to express the popular will. The armed forces broke up too. There were some important policy statements significant for the future – such as the creation of the Supreme Economic Council; nationalisation of the banks; founding of the ***Cheka***; banning of the Kadets; abolition of the courts; establishment of Revolutionary Tribunals; founding of the Red Army; repudiation of all foreign and domestic debts, as well as the introduction of the **Gregorian calendar** – but in truth the government was far from controlling events at this stage.

Key Terms

Cheka – the Secret Police originally established in December 1917 to break the strike of white-collar workers in government – civil servants, bank officials *et al*. Felix Dzerzhinsky organised them to destroy counter-revolutionaries and to shoot deserters. After the First World War the name was changed to OGPU as part of the Interior Ministry. The Secret Police was increasingly used to check on the loyalty of party members and to keep them compliant. As an arm of 'revolutionary justice' it operated outside soviet or party control, and was a weapon which brought fear and terror not just to Bolshevik enemies, but also to friends and to critics within the Bolshevik Party.

Gregorian calendar – Tsarist Russia used the 'old style' Julian calendar which was 13 days behind the 'new style' Gregorian calendar used by the other powers. The Gregorian calendar was introduced into Russia by the Bolsheviks in February 1918.

The peace of Brest-Litovsk, March 1918

At the beginning of 1918 opposition to the Bolsheviks was growing and it came to a head in March with the signing of the peace treaty. An armistice was signed with the Central Powers as early as 23 November 1917 and this was extended into January 1918. The Bolsheviks awaited revolutionary upheavals in Germany and elsewhere, but when these did not occur it became apparent that they could not stall the Germans forever. Trotsky adopted the slogan of 'neither peace nor war' but Lenin knew that there was now no Russian army to hold the Germans back. In February the Germans signed a separate peace with a puppet regime in the Ukraine and resumed the offensive. Finally, Lenin got his way and the Treaty of Brest-Litovsk was signed in March.

It was draconian: Russia lost 32 per cent of its arable land, 26 per cent of its railway system, 33 per cent of its factories, 75 per cent of coal and iron-ore mines and about 60 million citizens. No one had envisaged peace at such a price. Lenin alone was determined to accept. He argued that Russia had no choice and that the German war effort would collapse. He proved to be right on both counts – but in the short term the acceptance of the treaty greatly increased Bolshevik unpopularity and 12 days later the Left SRs left the government. Ironically the Communists, as the Bolsheviks now styled themselves, were saved by the onset of civil war. The alternative, the Whites, represented a return to the old regime; so the Communists, the Reds, were able to portray themselves as the saviours of the Revolution.

The Civil War

It is difficult to be precise about the actual start of the Civil War but historians are usually agreed that the rebellion of the Czech legions returning home (25 May 1918) and the attempted uprising of the Left SRs in July transformed the situation. By the summer of 1918 counter-revolutionary armies were forming in Siberia, the Ukraine and Estonia; nationalist movements had effective control in Finland, the Baltic States and Poland (these broke away permanently), the Ukraine, Georgia, Armenia and Azerbaijan (these were to be reconquered); and all the world's major powers had armed forces on Russian territory. At their lowest point the Reds only occupied about one-fifth of the old Russian Empire.

The Whites named Admiral Kolchak as Supreme Ruler in Omsk in November 1918 and by June 1919 Generals Yudenich in Estonia and Denikin in the south had acknowledged his leadership. The Reds had a particularly difficult year in 1919. Kolchak advanced as far as Ufa but was defeated in April 75 miles from the Volga region; Denikin reached Orel, 200 miles from Moscow, but fell back in October; while Yudenich actually entered the suburbs of Petrograd before being beaten off (also in October). As Figure 6 overleaf shows, the White Forces were never able to link up and they suffered a precipitate collapse in 1920. Kolchak was captured and executed, and Denikin resigned in favour of Peter Wrangel. He was able to revive White fortunes in the summer of 1920 as the Communists were thrown off guard by a Polish attack into the Ukraine (Poland had come into existence after the German collapse in November 1918). The Poles were beaten back and Wrangel's forces overcome so that by October 1920 the Civil War was effectively over. The foreign powers had also left by then, though the Japanese did not evacuate the Far East until 1922.

Dictatorship: the revolution betrayed

The Civil War is the context for the growth of Communist dictatorship and often its justification, but in truth the Communists were prepared to use any means to retain power regardless of whether or not there was civil war. In the absence of world revolution, Soviet Russia became the sole beacon of socialist hope. Therefore the regime had to survive at all costs, by any means. Moreover the Party was historically unique – it did not see itself as representative of anyone; it represented the truth – it was the locomotive of history. Anyone in opposition was quite simply wrong and should be crushed. The Party knew best; it had a messianic self-belief. It is ironic that the Civil War which was designed to overthrow the Communists probably enabled them to survive, because the Party was able to justify its extreme measures as a means of saving the revolution. Only gradually did the people become aware of the true nature of Bolshevism.

By mid 1918 the leadership realised it could not wait for the more advanced capitalist societies to become socialist. The Communist Party had to retain control by recreating central authority and it did this by reintroducing many traditional features of the old hierarchical system – a centralised police force, a proper army and so on. By June/July

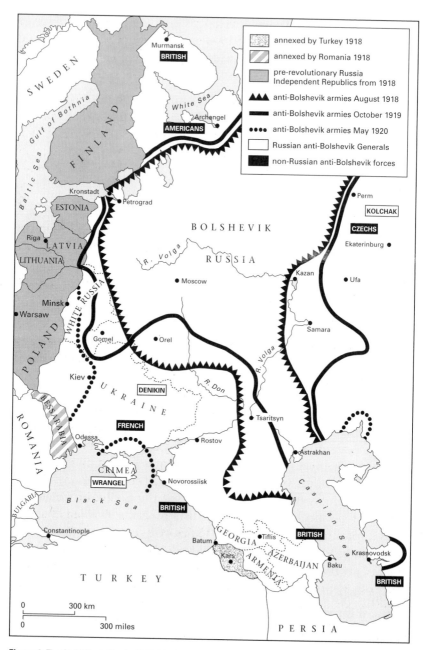

Figure 6 The Civil War in Russia 1918–20. Anti-Bolshevik forces controlled the Trans-Siberian railway from Kazan to Vladivostock.

Russia had in effect become a one-party state as elections were rigged or set aside and elected representatives of other parties were banned or arrested. But by using coercion the regime came to clash with the popular revolution, with the peasants and the workers.

In fact the regime was very soon at loggerheads with the **peasantry** as there was insufficient grain to feed the cities and the army. From the peasants' point of view there was little incentive to produce a surplus and there developed a serious town–country split over the issue. The popular revolution had given the peasants the land – they were content, but agricultural output fell. Lenin attempted a twin-track approach to the agrarian problem and both proved to be disastrous.

One was class warfare. The Communists were unsympathetic to the peasantry as a class, believing them to be *petit bourgeois* (*i.e.* capitalist), unlike the proletariat who were the leaders of the revolution. Thus Lenin tried to pitch poor peasants against supposedly rich ones (*kulaks*) but this was an artificial hypothesis and only succeeded in favouring unproductive peasants over productive ones.

The second aspect of policy was the forcible extraction of supposedly concealed stocks of grain. This policy was called 'food dictatorship' and was launched in May 1918. It was popular with town dwellers but the peasants were bewildered and obstructive, and responded with the slogan 'Down with the Communists. Long live the Bolsheviks!' Requisitioning, repression of the market, tax and conscription were all resisted. Peasants falsified their output returns, stopped cultivating, switched crops, concealed crops and even harvested at night! The government increased repression but output continued to fall (see table of statistics below). The sown area fell 17 per cent in 1919 and a further 11 per cent in 1920. Nevertheless, in the final analysis the peasants preferred the Reds to the Whites who were expected to return their land to the landowners. Peasants did give up grain and they did supply conscripts to the Red Army. Ultimately, peasant power prevailed. There was a terrible famine (1921–2) brought on by drought but made worse by Communist policy (5 million died) and the Communists were forced to change their economic policy from what was called '**War Communism**' to the New Economic Policy.

Tables of statistics

Production of cereal grain in Central Russia
(in millions of tons)

1913	78.2
1917	69.1
1920	48.2

Overall large-scale industrial production

1913	100
1917	77
1919	26
1920	18

Prices in Russia

1913	100
1917	755
1918	10,200
1919	92,300
1920	962,000
1921	8,190,000
1922	734,000,000

The Popular Revolution in the cities which had led to workers' control in the factories also proved disastrous as both experts – engineers, managers, accountants – as well as bosses were driven out. In fact, the industrial economy went into a dramatic freefall (see table of statistics). Factory production ceased. Total industrial output fell to around 20 per cent of prewar levels. There was 60 per cent unemployment in Petrograd in 1918 and workers abandoned the cities and went back to the countryside. The population of Petrograd dropped from 2.5 million in 1917 to 750,000 in 1920 (the population of Moscow halved). This represented a considerable thinning of the Communists' erstwhile supporters. The proletariat, which was meant to lead the revolution, was wasting away. In the absence of this support, the Party resorted increasingly to violence.

By the spring of 1918, Lenin realised that workers' control did not work. He advocated 'one-man management', a return to a disciplined system in which sloppy workers would be sacked and the others forced to work harder. This, in effect, represented a return to the old system: repressive bosses and workers with no voice. The workers' committees and unions became undemocratic agencies of government.

From the spring of 1918 the government resorted to the emergency measure of nationalisation, taking over factories or sectors of industry as they collapsed. In November 1920 measures were introduced to extend nationalisation to small businesses and workshops. This process developed into the idea of attempting to control the entire economy, signalled by the establishment of the State Planning Commission (Gosplan) in April 1921, which was designed to introduce large-scale electrification.

'The governmental system that emerged by 1921 was very different to the one outlined in the "April Theses". Soviet Russia had become a one-party state' (Read). The Party's attempts to control the peasants and workers had led to an enormous extension of political control and a transformation of the nature of the party. The system rapidly developed in the opposite direction anticipated by the people in October. Soviets were transformed – they met less frequently, were less representative and tended to carry out decisions passed down from on high rather than make them at grassroots level. They too became agencies of government. Opposition and the other remaining political parties were snuffed out by censorship, repression and violence, and as problems grew so did the secret police, the Cheka. From 120 employees in March 1918, the organisation grew to 143,000 in December 1921. The attempted coup by the Left SRs in July 1918 and the serious wounding of Lenin in August led to a more systematic use of violence, a period known as the **'Red Terror'**. There followed a vast number of arrests and 6,300 official executions took place up to the end of 1918 (not including the Tsar and his family who were shot in July) and the pace continued into 1919. If anything the pressure increased after the end of the Civil War, wiping out the remnants of the popular movement in 1920 and 1921. By the end of 1920 there were some 50,000 inmates in Soviet concentration camps.

Expanding repression and control led to ever-expanding bureaucratisation. As the Communist Party developed a managerial and administrative apparatus to control every aspect of life, it had to recruit on a large scale so that by 1921 party membership had risen to 732,000. But these career bureaucrats were rarely true Marxist revolutionaries and 'the dilution of the Party by less reliable recruits was best combated by more centralisation and discipline' (Read). At the Eighth Party Congress in March 1919 it was declared that 'all decisions of the higher echelons are absolutely binding for those below' and prescribed more written reports; more intervention from above; more discipline; more centralisation; more control; and purges – in fact, the Party was reduced by half by 1923. Large-scale propaganda was to be developed to raise class consciousness both among the people and within the party.

However, although the Communists had been successful in winning the Civil War, snuffing out opposition and establishing their political control, the people had had to pay a terrible price – it is estimated 10 million persons died between 1917 and 1921 (5 million in the famine, over 2 million in combat and over 2 million from disease). With the emergence of opposition at the end of the Civil War in the form of strikes and peasant risings on an unprecedented scale, and with the continuing collapse of the economy, even Lenin recognised that there was a need to change direction.

The New Economic Policy

The previous three years' policy of grain requisitioning and wholesale nationalisation was described by Lenin as 'War Communism' in 1921. The policy had failed and Lenin clearly tried to show that it had only been brought into being to cope with the extreme conditions of the Civil War. However, this was not true. It had been the chosen policy of the Party, regardless of the Civil War, but it was clear that it had not worked. Grain requisitioning had led to less production and widespread famine, and nationalisation had not halted the decline of industry. Extreme inflation had led to the virtual disappearance of the money economy – by October 1920 the rouble was 1 per cent of its 1917 value – and falling food production and peasant revolts (such as the drawn-out Tambov rebellion a few hundred miles south-east of Moscow) convinced Lenin that he needed to change course. He decided upon the New Economic Policy in February 1921. Because of the **Kronstadt Mutiny** in late February, Lenin was able to persuade the Party to accept it at the Tenth Congress.

The sailors of Kronstadt – those erstwhile supporters of the Bolshevik Revolution – wanted a relaxation of Communist control now that the Civil War was over. They wanted an end to ballot rigging; freedom of the press and so on – in short, a return to the revolutionary principles of 1917. The Communists were shaken but reacted with deadly force throwing 50,000 soldiers against the sailors and extinguishing the revolt in just over two weeks. It was clear there was to be no political relaxation and the crushing of the revolt 'represents the poignant end of the popular revolution. The vibrant force of grassroots democracy had been finally destroyed by one of its products – Bolshevism' (Read).

At the **Tenth Party Congress** in March 1921 Lenin announced two important policies:
- the end of factionalism;
- the New Economic Policy.

1   Although political debate had been eliminated in Russian society it had still continued within the Communist Party. Now Lenin decided it must stop: 'we have allowed ourselves the luxury of discussions and disputes . . . discussion means disputes; disputes means discord; discord means that the Communists have become weak'. This was to be the prelude to an important tightening up of party discipline.

2   'On the replacement of the requisitions with a tax in kind' was the resolution introducing the NEP. By taking a percentage of output, this would allow the peasants to dispose of their surplus. Thus the legitimate return of private trade, of the market, of capitalism, had to be accepted. In truth, the NEP did little more than sanction the methods of trade already in existence. The peasants achieved a great victory; their revolution had been successful (though it would be extinguished after 1928 by Stalin). The readmission of private enterprise into industry was also accepted; the 'commanding heights' (heavy industry, banking and foreign trade) were retained by the government but small-scale manufacture was returned to private management and expected to make a profit. All this led to the re-use of money and in 1922 a new rouble was introduced to stabilise the currency and the State Bank was to provide credit. By 1923 the NEP was responsible for three-quarters of all retail trade and by 1926 the economy had almost regained the production

levels of 1913. The NEP was seen as temporary but Lenin envisaged that it would be in operation for some time.

The climbdown on the economic front was accompanied not only by increased discipline within the Party but with greater control over society at large. After the Congress, censorship was regularised, the GPU was established as a permanent political police force to replace the 'temporary' Cheka (February 1922), political prisons became permanent and expanded their intake (the number of camps grew from 84 in 1920 to 315 by 1923), show trials of clergy and SRs took place and universities lost their autonomy. Any echoes of the popular revolution that remained after this were to be swept away during the 'second revolution' of 1928–31, but by then Lenin was long gone.

The death of Lenin

Lenin was shot in the neck by an SR, Fannie Kaplan, in August 1918, but he made a remarkable recovery (despite the fact that the bullet was not removed), and his health was good for the next two years. During 1921, however, he suffered from headaches and insomnia and by spring 1922 he accepted that he was ill and scaled down his involvement in the day-to-day running of affairs (his doctors removed the bullet in April).

On 25 May 1922 Lenin suffered his first stroke which put him out of action for two months, but he resumed full-time work in October. However, on 15 December he suffered a second stroke, and a third six days later. Sensing that the end was near, Lenin dictated his 'Testament' between 23 and 26 December, with an addendum on 4 January 1923. In this document he assessed (or rather criticised) potential successors, without naming an heir. He identified Trotsky as the most capable but overconfident and not a team player; Kamenev and Zinoviev he condemned for their opposition in 1917; Stalin, he recommended in the postscript, should be dismissed because he was 'too coarse'.

On 10 March 1923 Lenin suffered another massive stroke which left him literally speechless. For the last 10 months of his life he was to all intents and purposes, a living corpse. He died on 21 January 1924 and the collective leadership which had come into being since the onset of his illness (principally Zinoviev, Kamenev and Stalin – Trotsky was already isolated), was able to suppress his 'Testament'. The next four years would witness a battle for power which, surprisingly, was won by Stalin. Lenin himself was embalmed, put on display (as indeed he still is today) and subsequently enjoyed veneration bordering on deification – until 1991, that is. Clearly however, at Lenin's death the Bolsheviks had held on to power and consolidated their position in the most difficult circumstances. This was Lenin's achievement.

Analysis

So, how were the Bolsheviks able to hold on to, and consolidate, their power? It would probably be helpful to break our answer down into five elements:

◢ The Bolsheviks' self-belief and ruthless determination
◢ The atomisation of the opposition
◢ The support they were able to generate
◢ The Civil War (probably the crucial factor)
◢ The concessions to a mixed economy (the NEP).

1 As we have already indicated, the Bolsheviks displayed a messianic self-belief – a supreme confidence that they knew best, that history was on their side. They were motivated by utopianism, by a desire to transform the world, by a vision of world socialism. If people did not agree they would have to be educated, their consciousness would have to be raised. All this translated into a ruthless determination to hold on to power at all costs. To do this the Bolsheviks restored a narrow, centralised, elitist, authoritarian government backed by force, terror and bureaucratic control. It was not dissimilar to the old Tsarist system but it turned out to be much more cruel. The Bolsheviks had no compunction about shooting striking workers or obstructive peasants. Thus they did not see themselves as the servants of the people but their teachers. Yet they came to power with the backing of a considerable proportion of the population who believed they would carry out the popular programme. Only gradually did the Bolsheviks reveal their true colours as appointments replaced elections, directives took the place of discussion, and other parties were edged out. That the Communists were able to dupe the people, set themselves against the people and hold on to power is a remarkable achievement and much of the credit (if that is the right word) for this goes to Lenin.

Although Marxism, with its emphasis on irresistible economic and social forces, plays down the role of the individual in history, there is no doubt that Lenin's contribution to Bolshevik success was crucial. He held the Party together and was able to dominate his quarrelsome colleagues. He had the lucky knack of getting things right – he was right about the seizure of power, he was right about the collapse of the Germans and his near-miraculous recovery from the assassination attempt in 1918 gave him unrivalled authority. But his contribution was perhaps not as great as subsequent Soviet historiography made out. Moreover it is clear that any attempt to whitewash his character and contrast his 'kindness' with Stalin's cruelty will not succeed. 'Stalin's course . . . [was] . . . charted by Lenin' (Pipes). Dictatorship and terror were the product of Lenin's tutelage. Thousands of 'class enemies' were executed; thousands more were thrown into camps. Lenin was a ruthless dictator. In truth he had little contact with, or sympathy for, ordinary people, despite his politics – after all, he was not a peasant himself, nor was he a worker – he was a product of the bourgeoisie. However, dictatorship and terror alone were not enough to ensure Bolshevik success.

2   Bolshevism also survived because 'the processes which atomised its constituency of 1917 also prevented the emergence of a coherent popular movement against it' (Acton). Basically what happened was that the country fell apart, economically, socially and geographically – and this enabled the Bolsheviks to hold on. Russia suffered an economic collapse on the scale of a modern Black Death and in the aftermath the alliance between workers, soldiers and peasants also fell apart. The army simply disintegrated. Hostility developed between city and countryside as hungry workers came to favour the forcible requisitioning of peasant grain. At the same time, economic collapse caused problems within the countryside and within the city. The struggle for grain set region against region, village against village and peasant against peasant. Workers too were pitted against each other in the fight for jobs and bread. Thus there was no united front against the regime. Indeed the government was able to take advantage of this to gain the support of one group against another.

In addition, the opposition on the Left – the SRs – was weak and divided, and hampered by a fear of betraying the revolution and forfeiting the gains made. They colluded in the demise of the Kadets and their own belated rising in the summer of 1918 was not so much a *coup d'état* as a *coup de théâtre* – the SRs were only playing at revolution. Opponents found that the only alternative was to side with the Whites who represented counter-revolution, a return to the old order. For many this was not an attractive choice.

3   To return to the issue of support, it is also quite clear that despite their betrayal of many of the principles of 1917 the Bolsheviks were able to retain sufficient support to survive. The regime could benefit some sections of society. The struggle for survival led different cities, villages, workers or peasants who were at a disadvantage locally to call on the government to intervene on their behalf. Where it did so, it gained allies. It came to be seen as a source of food. This process enabled the regime 'to establish a new basis of authority which rested no longer on mass support but on a combination of force and patronage' (Acton). In addition, an ambivalence was created by the regime's propaganda – that is to say the government said it stood for the revolution, it said it stood for the workers and this made it difficult for many to contemplate active opposition.

Finally, it was an important source of employment. As the Party's administrative apparatus expanded so too did job opportunities. Jobs meant survival and to climb up the party hierarchy brought social mobility too. Thus the bureaucrats had a vested interest in the maintenance of the regime – and many of the recruits were erstwhile activists who now left the people leaderless. Indeed from being a mass party of workers, the Party became a body of officials. By 1922 over two-thirds of the Party were administrators and these people were quite happy to accept orders from the top. However, this support was still very narrow and shrinking which leads most historians to conclude that without the Civil War the regime would probably have been overthrown.

4   It is perhaps a great irony that the Civil War, which was designed to overthrow the Bolsheviks, proved to be their salvation. Because the Whites were committed to reversing the gains that the peasants

and workers had made, the Reds were seen as the lesser of two evils. As the Whites came to be identified more and more with the reactionary military officer class, the Bolsheviks came to be seen as the only alternative to a restoration of Tsarist society. Thus although the peasants detested the Reds, they loathed the Whites more and this was what saved the regime. The vast majority of Russians wanted a socialist settlement and the Communist mutation was the only one on offer. But how did the Communists survive the Civil War? After all, they were faced with nationalist secession, foreign intervention (the British, French, Americans and Japanese among others) as well as three White armies (and non-aligned forces).

First of all the Whites were weak; their armies not very large. For instance, Denikin's army consisted of only around 100,000 men at most and when Yudenich advanced into Petrograd in September 1919 he only had about 14,400 men at his disposal – hardly enough to hold such a large city. The Red Army, on the other hand, numbered millions. Although they controlled the grain areas, the Whites had great difficulty recruiting and enormous problems with desertion. Moreover they lacked a secure base area and had considerable difficulties with communication and coordination. For example, Denikin on the Black Sea could only communicate with Kolchak in the Urals via Paris. And their forces never did link up. They never fought as a unit; they were too dispersed. In addition, there were enormous political differences – from monarchism at one end of the spectrum to liberal democracy at the other. The execution of the Tsar and his family dealt a blow to monarchism but the generals were little inclined to a parliamentary solution. In fact, the White movement became more authoritarian and conservative and therefore less appealing to the population at large, as time passed. The moderates were squeezed out and this increasing polarisation worked to the Reds' advantage. The Whites' Russian nationalism did not find much of an echo in the non-Russian periphery where they operated. The Whites were not a viable political alternative.

Foreign intervention was also not as formidable as it might first appear. Logistically, it was limited and the foreign powers had relatively narrow objectives. For instance, Britain and France intervened to keep Russia in the war against Germany but once the

Germans were defeated, war-weariness prevented any real continuation. The most formidable interventionist group, the Czechs, were only accidental participants and their main aim was to get out and get home. However, they did force the Communists to tackle the formation of the Red Army in earnest.

The Reds, on the other hand, enjoyed a number of distinct advantages. They controlled the Russian heartland which contained 60 million people, the remnants of industry, military stockpiles and internal lines of communication. They controlled Petrograd and Moscow; a large part of the rail network (along which most campaigns were fought) connected to these cities. In addition, Trotsky created the Red Army which quickly built up to 1.5 million men in 1919 and to 3.5 million by mid 1920. Despite a high desertion rate, the White army could never match these numbers. And because the Whites and rebel nationalities were so widely dispersed, the Reds could pick off their opponents one by one. Yet it took nearly three years, of tough fighting complicated by the Polish campaign, for the outcome – a Red victory – to be decided.

The Civil War had been a great opportunity for the Bolsheviks to create the authoritarian regime they needed to survive and it had enabled them to mould society along the lines they considered appropriate. However, the ending of the Civil War was seen by many as a hoped-for opportunity for the oppression to be relaxed. When this did not occur the Communists were faced with a wave of rebellions. Lenin's solution was compromise.

5   The final factor that enabled the Communists to survive – despite the fact that they only had the support of a tiny minority of the population – was the step back from socialism and the reintroduction of capitalism in the form of the New Economic Policy. This worked: peasant uprisings virtually ceased, the economy recovered and the Communist regime was thereby consolidated. In effect, capitalism had never really gone away – without the black market the people of Russia could not have survived. By introducing the NEP Lenin acknowledged this. However, there was to be no political relaxation; in fact, political control was tightened up, and the large number of arrests in 1921

and 1922 finished off the opposition on the Left – just as the Civil War had dealt with the Right.

Conclusion

It would appear that Russia (or the Union of Soviet Socialist Republics as it was called from 1922) had come full circle. After a brief explosion of democracy the authoritarian bureaucratic Tsarist police state had been replaced by the authoritarian bureaucratic Communist police state. However, there had been massive economic and social change. By 1920 the aristocracy, the church hierarchy, landowners, property owners, capitalists, bankers, entrepreneurs, merchants, industrialists and large-scale traders had all disappeared – either they had died or been driven out. A total of 2 million *emigrés* had settled outside of Russia by 1921, including many of the most talented, skilled and educated people – a loss which would cause problems for a generation. All the main institutions of the *ancien regime* had gone too – monarchy, the legal system, police, army, navy, State Council, Duma; and all the factories, banks, commercial and financial enterprises, mines and transport had been expropriated, nationalised or destroyed. Attitudes to money and property had altered profoundly and the 'numerically small but socially divisive tip of the social pyramid had been wiped away' (Read).

In addition, a new form of government had come into being offering an alternative economic system to that which prevailed in the rest of the world. It was a system that purported to be a world system and it actively advocated the overthrow of foreign governments and societies – the Comintern was set up for this very purpose in 1919. Indeed since 1917 the Communist system has acted as an inspiration for some and as a source of confrontation for others. Even into the 1980s the Soviet Union represented a formidable opponent and alternative to western, capitalist society. However, once Mikhail Gorbachev removed coercion from the system, the Russian people were happy to throw off communism in a very short space of time – despite over 70 years of political education and propaganda. In truth, the regime never did deliver the principles of 1917 and the Russian people are still in search of them today.

TASKS

Notemaking: a few tips

As you are probably already aware, notemaking is the foundation of all your study activity. The notes you make act as a shorthand to remind you what you have read and they also (often) form the basis for essay writing and (usually) for revision. Moreover, notemaking makes reading an active process as you are required to concentrate and extract the most important points.

The two most common errors when notemaking are either to write out too much – there is no point in writing out practically the whole book – or too little – thereby missing out important points. Proper notemaking requires you to think hard about what is relevant and this can be quite difficult when you are unfamiliar with a topic.

Another useful tip is to ensure that your notes are easy on the eye. A densely-packed set of words is rather off-putting when it is time for revision. It is important to space out your notes and to break up the pages with gaps (these can be useful for extra points later). Always indent, and use headings, sub-headings, numbered points, underlining, colours, *etc*. Above all, make your notes interesting.

Making notes on this chapter

A) Summary of events
  i) Early days
  ii) Peace of Brest-Litovsk
  iii) The Civil War
  iv) Dictatorship: the revolution betrayed
    a) peasantry
    b) workers
    c) Red Terror
  v) The New Economic Policy
  vi) The death of Lenin
B) Analysis
  i) The Bolsheviks' self-belief
  ii) The atomisation of the opposition
  iii) Support
  iv) The Civil War
  v) NEP
C) Conclusion

CHAPTER SEVEN

OLD MYTHS DIE HARD: THE HISTORIOGRAPHY OF THE RUSSIAN REVOLUTION

Objectives

◢ To make the historiography of the Russian Revolution more understandable

◢ To examine historians' current position.

There is no topic in history that has been more distorted by political historiography than the Russian Revolution. Until the recent collapse of the Soviet Union it was something of a political football kicked back and forth between East and West. Accordingly, various political interpretations made a complex event even more complex and current historians are having to peal away layers of myth to get closer to the truth. One of the main problems has been the inaccessibility of source material, but since Gorbachev the archives have been partially opened up. We are finally achieving, if not consensus, then at least greater clarity.

Thus you are warned that the subject's historiography is a minefield. Fortunately Professor Edward Acton in his 1990 book *Rethinking the Russian Revolution* has at least made the topic more understandable. In this work he concentrated on four traditions of interpretation:

◢ the Orthodox Soviet view
◢ the liberal (western) view
◢ the libertarian (left) view
◢ revisionism.

Four approaches

1 From its inception the **Soviet** State was concerned to propagate its own version of events which emphasised Lenin's genius, the Bolsheviks' infallible leadership and the inevitability of what happened – and what happened was a process of class conflict leading to the overthrow of capitalist exploitation by the party representing progressive socialism. All of this ushered in the dictatorship of the proletariat. The great bulk of the archival

material that was selected for publication was to support this view and what did not fit was locked away.

2 The western **Liberal** view, on the other hand, was an outright rejection of the Soviet interpretation, of irresistible economic and social forces, of class conflict, of historical inevitability. The liberal view saw the revolution as fortuitous, the result of the coincidence of a disastrous war, abysmal leadership and inept politicians. Thus the liberal approach focused on politics and the leading actors in the historical drama, and subordinated the role of the masses. The Bolsheviks were seen as a ruthless, conspiratorial group of fanatics who exploited chaos to capture power.

3 The Libertarian view tended to concentrate on the aspirations of the ordinary people who were betrayed by the Bolsheviks. For the libertarians, it was the masses who swept away Tsarism, and the Bolsheviks who crushed the masses. 'Protest which Soviet historians disparage as 'spontaneous' and unreflecting, and which liberal historians see as merciless and destructive, libertarians see as [a constructive attempt by] the . . . masses to assert direct control over their lives.' (Acton)

However, much of libertarian work was unprofessional and therefore did not gain wide acceptance.

4 **Revisionism** has sought to subject all received wisdom to scrutiny. In particular, western historians in the 1960s and 1970s questioned the liberal account, and placed greater emphasis on research into economic, social and institutional aspects of the revolution. They too began to look at the aspirations of ordinary men and women, at the political parties, at the Tsarist economy, at the dynamics of popular unrest under Nicholas II, and at the drama of 1917 itself.

◢ Source

One implication of revisionist work is that the root cause both of the fall of Tsarism and the failure of the liberals and moderate socialists, lies much deeper than the liberal interpretation would have it. Another is that the view of October as the product of a truly mass-revolutionary movement is not so wide of the mark.

Edward Acton, **Rethinking the Russian Revolution** (Arnold, 1980)

An example: the October Revolution

Let us see how these interpretations differ in practice by looking at the October Revolution.

1 According to the Soviet view, Lenin correctly assessed that class conflict within Russia rendered it ripe for socialist revolution according to Marxist analysis. The Bolshevik success was based on the support of the majority of the population whose raised consciousness was the product of a sustained campaign of propaganda and education by the vanguard party, the Bolsheviks. Lenin then chose his moment with consummate skill and directed an armed insurrection against the government. The swift spread of Soviet power after the October Revolution was 'in the truest sense democratic and popular, the political expression and culmination of explosive class struggle' (Acton).

2 In the Liberal view, the Bolshevik victory was not popular and democratic. The Bolsheviks were a highly centralised body of ruthless revolutionaries who were able to take advantage of the anarchy that followed the February Revolution. Bolshevik support was very narrow and the key to their success was their infiltration of the various committees. Lenin was, above all, an opportunist whose political programme consisted of promising something for everyone; whereas in fact he had no intention of delivering any of it. The October Revolution was simply a *coup d'état* by Lenin whose principal aim was to secure power and never let it go.

3 In the Libertarian view, the revolution was truly popular but the Bolsheviks 'were the illegitimate beneficiaries of the autonomous action of the masses' (Acton). Time and again the professional revolutionaries were taken by surprise by the popular revolution from below – a revolution that was creative and constructive, but it was taken over by the political parties and the Bolsheviks were the most ruthless, most organised and most able to exploit the masses. They did so by deception, 'by skilfully [echoing] the aspirations of the masses . . . the masses' challenge had been sufficient to sweep away Tsarism and nobility, to dispossess the bourgeoisie and all but destroy the existing state. But it proved unable to prevent the reassertion of authority in a guise less

easy to expose than Tsarism or capitalism but no less oppressive: Bolshevism' (Acton).

4 Revisionism has demonstrated that all three approaches are inadequate though in many respects it has much in common with the libertarian approach by emphasising the need to see events 'from below'. The collapse of authority gave the aspirations of soldiers, workers and peasants free reign and the actions of ordinary people rendered the Provisional Government impotent. The Bolsheviks gained support because their view coincided with that of the masses; they also gained support because they were initially tolerant, flexible and prepared to defy as well as follow Lenin. The Party stepped into a vacuum in October but by identifying with Soviet power it did so with much goodwill. This was soon forfeited as the Party came to rely on coercion.

The position today

With the collapse of the Soviet Union, the revolution is now truly history rather than part of present-day politics. This should in future bring a more dispassionate, less partisan approach to the subject.

When Gorbachev came to power in 1985 he sought to establish continuity with Lenin and to encourage critical analysis of Stalin. However, this backfired as historians came to see the continuity between Lenin and Stalin, and criticised Lenin too. Since the demise of Communism, Russian historians have turned their attention to the question 'what went wrong in 1917?' What happened to democracy? Also, there is much interest in Tsarist Russia, the Duma, the political parties and the Provisional Government.

Western historiography, on the other hand, has been dominated by a revival of the liberal approach in the form of two blockbuster volumes by Professor Richard Pipes: *The Russian Revolution* (1990) running to nearly 950 pages, and *Russia under the Bolshevik Regime* (1994), slightly less foreboding at just under 600 pages. These works, the former in particular, are meticulously researched and very well written. They are also a mine of useful information and can be used as a quarry. Professor Pipes has produced a concise history, a synthesis of the two books in just over 400 pages, which was published in 1995.

In these volumes, personalities and politics return to centre stage and great stress is placed on the continuity between the Tsarist and Bolshevik regimes. However, Pipes is not interested in the peasants and workers, and the 'revolution from below' gets short shrift. Consequently, Geoffrey Hosking, in a very useful review in the *Times Literary Supplement* (1 February 1991), suggested that the first volume is not quite the comprehensive view of the revolution that the preface promises. It is not the sole guide to the events it describes, but it is well worth reading.

In order to compensate for some of the gaps in Pipes's approach, you would do well to turn to Christopher Read's *From Tsar to Soviets* (1996) with the telling subtitle – 'The Russian people and their revolution, 1917–21'. In this work, the experience of ordinary men and women are restored to centre stage and are shown to have been important in creating the events of 1917. This is surely the way forward for the historiography of the revolution, which will ultimately lead to a better understanding of how events 'from below' interacted with the personalities at the top, in government.

There was a real revolution in Russia in 1917, a brief flicker of liberty but it was soon extinguished.

◢ Source

The tragedy of the revolution lies in the Bolsheviks' failure to recognise the real revolution of the time and instead to pursue their own highly-structured presuppositions about what the revolution should have been like and what the chief actors should have been doing. While they certainly incorporated an important part of the popular revolution they were also blind to other aspects and violently repressed parts of it that they neither liked nor understood.

Christopher Read, ***From Tsar to Soviets – The Russian People and their Revolution 1917–21*** *(UCL Press, 1996)*

But if the opportunity of 1917 was soon lost let us hope that the opportunity presented to the Russian people after 1991 is not.

FURTHER READING

This is a deliberately short, selective bibliography as it is recognised that students do not have the time to read more than a few works. If you wish to pursue some aspect of these events in detail, note that many of the books cited here have extensive bibliographies.

There are a number of short works on the Russian Revolution like this one, but these have not been included as after reading one short work a student should be looking for depth of knowledge rather than more of the same.

Sources

There are two useful works edited by Martin McCauley:

Octobrists to Bolsheviks. Imperial Russia 1905–1917 (Edward Arnold, 1984)

The Russian Revolution and the Soviet State 1917–1921 (Macmillan, 1980)

The following appeared too late for this book, but has been well received:

Andrei Maylunas and Sergei Mironenko *A Lifelong Passion: Nicholas and Alexandra – Their Own Story* (Weidenfeld and Nicolson, 1996) which features their correspondence over 34 years.

Historiography

Edward Acton *Rethinking the Russian Revolution* (Arnold, 1990). Very useful – see chapter 7 of this book.

The wider context

There are three volumes in the Longman History of Russia series that are relevant:

Donald Saunders *Russia in the age of Reaction and Reform – 1801–81* (1992)

Hans Rogger *Russia in the age of Modernisation and Revolution 1881–1917* (1983)

Martin McCauley *The Soviet Union 1917–1991* (1993)

Biography

Dominic Lieven *Nicholas II – Emperor of all the Russias* (John Murray, 1993) – an attempt to see the Tsar in a more sympathetic light.

Beryl Williams *Lenin* (1997) in the Longman Profiles in Power series but not seen at the time of writing.

Tsarist Russia

Abraham Ascher *The Revolution of 1905, vol. 1* (Stanford, 1988) and *vol. 2* (Standford, 1992) – very detailed.

Peter Gatrell *The Tsarist Economy 1850–1917* (Batsford, 1986)

Richard Pipes *Russia under the Old Regime* (Weidenfeld and Nicolson, 1974)

The Revolution

Richard Pipes *The Russian Revolution 1899–1919* (Collins Harvill, 1990)

Richard Pipes *Russia under the Bolshevik Regime* (Harvill, 1994)

Christopher Read *From Tsar to Soviets – The Russian people and their revolution, 1917–21* (University College London Press, 1996)

(The above are discussed in chapter 7.)

James D. White *The Russian Revolution* (Edward Arnold, 1994)

The following appeared too late for this book but has been well reviewed:

Orlando Figes A People's Tragedy: *The Russian Revolution 1891–1924* (Jonathan Cape, 1996)

Tape

Clive Castaldo *Russia in Revolution 1894–1924* (Fast Forward, 1995) – very useful with lots of quotes from Pipes.

For the coffee table

Peter Kurth *Tsar – The Lost World of Nicholas and Alexandra* (Little, Brown and Co., 1995) – a sumptuous production with a wealth of glossy photographs.

INDEX

KEY TERMS

MAIN INDEX

Longman History in Depth
Series editor: Christopher Culpin

Titles in the series

Addison Wesley Longman Limited,
Edinburgh Gate, Harlow,
Essex CM20 2JE, England
and Associated Companies throughout the world.

First published 1998

Set in 9.5/13pt Stone Serif
Produced by Longman Singapore Publisher Pte Ltd
Printed in Singapore

ISBN 0 582 29731 1

Acknowledgements

We are grateful to Macmillan Press Ltd for permission to reproduce an extract from *The Russian Revolution and the Soviet State* by Martin McCauley (1975).

The publishers are grateful to the David King Collection for supplying all the photographs in this book.

Cover photograph: Petrograd's armed workers pose at the armoured vehicle *Lieutenant Schmidt* in October 1917. Society for Cooperation in Russian and Soviet Studies.

The publisher's policy is to use paper manufactured from sustainable forests.